Caught in
The Crossfire

Caught in The Crossfire

The Unjust Degradation of a Highly Decorated Military Officer

Levonda Joey Selph

Prominent Books

Writing, Editing, Book Layout & Cover Design by:
Writer Services, LLC (WriterServices.net)

ISBN10: 0-9800705-8-9
ISBN13: 978-0-9800705-8-3

Prominent Books and the Prominent Books logo are
property of Prominent Books, LLC.

TABLE OF CONTENTS

DEDICATION

I want to dedicate this work to Anna Modesto. I am sincerely grateful to the Veteran's Medical Center in Memphis, Tennessee where I received the best medical care for Post Traumatic Stress Disorder (PTSD). This is where I had the honor of meeting Dr. Modesto. She is one amazing person who helped me get through the toughest time in my life. She helped me to recognize what is important in life and how to deal with what is not important. It was that which is not important to my future that caused me the most mental and emotional pain imaginable. Dr. Modesto helped me to recognize why my life was worthy and how to cope with the past tragedies that brought my career to an end and my life to an all time low.

I also wish to dedicate this work to my loyal friends who have stuck by me throughout my journey of the good and bad. Specifically, John Hess – San Francisco, California; Albert Skroch, Jr. – The Villages, Florida; George Tangy – Phoenix, Arizona; Robert Brown – Jonesboro, Arkansas; Nancy Morgan – Cabot, Arkansas; Myra Miller – Silver Springs, Maryland; Dana "Wilson" Cory – Fairfax, Virginia; Karin Mari – Fort Meyers, Florida; Bill Richey – Jacksonville, Florida; Joshua Holland – Crystal

River, Florida; and last, my family who put up with me and my career choice that took me away from them for thirty years. These are my friends and family who have been there for me—always.

Finally, I would be remiss if I did not mention my constant companion—my unconditional love—my chihuahua Buffy. Buffy has been my saving grace. She demands nothing of me and accepts me just as I am. She is the most precious thing I have known in my life, and I love her dearly.

INTRODUCTION

I grew up with a strong work ethic and an understanding of what it means to be honest. I joined the military in my early twenties, served for 30-years, moved up in the ranks, and received over thirty-six citations, decorations and medals, which includes two bronze stars. In addition, I have over forty-seven coins given to me by General Officers and other senior Army leaders. I have one from Strom Thurman, former Senator from South Carolina (now deceased), all for a job well done in various assignments. I served my country in the Persian Gulf and in Iraq honorably and with dedication to my work. I was married to the military and extremely proud of my accomplishments.

Now, at the end of my career, I sit here as a beaten down woman by the very country I had served and believed in for so many years. I can't help but feel angry, sad and disillusioned by what has transpired. In their efforts to bring down someone else, the Department of Justice destroyed everything I worked for over my long and esteemed career. Overnight, my career was tarnished along with my flawless reputation.

It is because of these injustices that I feel I was compelled to write this book of my story—that of a woman who grew up in great poverty, joined the military with wide-eyed enthusiasm, only to be tossed aside three decades later without even a thank you for putting my life on the line many times and helping my country protect its values.

This is my story, and I hope those who read it will come to know how thankless our very own government can be to those who have served with selfless service.

CHAPTER 1

REGARDED AS THE ENEMY

CHAPTER 1

REGARDED AS THE ENEMY

I have to assume it was a typical Saturday morning. I really wouldn't know because I wasn't yet awake when I heard the doorbell ringing. And little did I know that once I opened the door, my life would be changed forever.

Living alone in the Washington D.C. area, and being pretty much a workaholic, I didn't get too many visitors, especially not on a Saturday at 7:30 in the morning.

Living near the beltway, I tried to get out on weekday mornings by 5:30 to avoid the usual beltway traffic. I figured I could either sit in traffic or be at my office doing something productive, so I'd opt to get in early and then stay until nearly 7 pm each night to avoid the agonizing chaos on Route 66. Since that was my normal Monday through Friday routine, Saturday was a day I looked forward to sleeping in until 9 am. But not on this particular Saturday, which was on March 3, 2007.

I got up quickly, put on my robe and dashed downstairs to see who was at the door. I could see through the peep-hole that there was one man holding up his badge, so I opened the door. He told me immediately that he was with the United States Army Criminal Investigation Command—usually abbreviated as just CID. They are the United States Military's law enforcement agency responsible for the conduct of criminal investigations—somewhat like the Federal Bureau of Investigation. He also told me that he was acting in an official capacity. He was one of seven men and women at the door, and they wanted to search the premises and ask me some questions.

I didn't think I had anything to hide, so I let them in to do whatever they deemed necessary. Before any questioning began, I was told that I could have an attorney present if I needed one. However, not knowing why they were here, and not having any knowledge that I had done anything wrong, I declined. So, two of the agents took me into one of my bedrooms upstairs and began asking questions about what I did during my time spent in Iraq.

I was a logistics officer in Iraq from June 2003 through October 2005. It was now 2007, and I had been stateside for nearly two years. I had no idea what they were trying to find out, but I answered the questions as they were asked. They wanted to know specifics about what I did, where I was living while I was over there, and whom I was in contact with in great detail. They kept asking question after question for hours, and I continued answering all the same, providing them with whatever I could remember.

The main theme of the questions centered around one of the contractors I worked with while I was over in Iraq. Thinking that I had nothing to hide, I didn't know what they wanted to find out, but I knew from other sources that he (the contractor) was under some kind of investigation. I also knew that he had been arrested in January 2007 and held in jail in Kuwait City, Kuwait. I had no knowledge of any wrongdoing on his part, but apparently they had reason to believe or found out something about him that led to this interrogation.

The contractor was a man in his seventies; very successful. He was the President of American Logistics Services, as well as Lee Dynamics International, a Kuwaiti-based, American-owned Company, or so I thought. I had met him in Iraq and worked with his employees in 2004–2005.

Meanwhile, as the questioning continued, the other agents were turning my house topsy-turvy. One of my sergeants, back in the fall of 2006, told me there was a rumor circulating that I was under investigation, but I told him that I didn't know anything about it, and did not care because I had done nothing wrong. I sent a note to the contractor with whom I had known to see if he had heard of any such investigation. Apparently, the sergeant was right.

Even before I could straighten up my house, the questioning continued at my office located in the National Guard Bureau in Arlington, Virginia. Again, they asked questions primarily about my relationship with this contractor and again I answered to the best of my ability, telling them whatever I could. The office was also turned topsy-turvy. This went on for hours and was wearing me down. The questioning on the 3rd of March 2007 continued nonstop for eleven hours.

The following week, I was called in and questioned again, this time by the DOJ (Department of Justice). The questions were similar to those asked by the CID.

At this point, the deputy in my division told me that I should get a lawyer. I was still thinking I had done noth-

5

ing wrong, but decided to follow his advice and started asking around to see if anyone I knew could recommend a good attorney.

As chief of an inspection team, my job at this time had me traveling a lot. The team and I would travel for a week at a time, and look at various units for logistics policy compliance and combat readiness. We would then write a report followed by briefing to the local Command, normally with the presence of a General Officer on Friday mornings, prior to our departure back to Arlington, Virginia. We would then return home on Friday and have most of the weekend off before going to the office or back out on another trip on Sunday or Monday.

The DOJ began questioning me between trips, again firing questions for eight to ten hours or more at a stretch. This went on at least a dozen times, and each time, I would leave in tears followed by sleepless nights. I felt as if I was being interrogated as one would interrogate a terrorist.

I later read in the media that the Chief of the Department of Justice had approved the same interrogation tactics used on terrorists to achieve information from suspects.

Here I was, a highly decorated member of the United States Military for over 30 years, and I was being treated like a terrorist. The worst part was that I still had no idea why. Anywhere from three to seven people, including CID agents and DOJ prosecutors would be in the room with me at any given time, trying hard to get me to confess to something or tell them some secret that I had not yet told them. It was frustrating and demoralizing because I had no new answers beyond what I'd been saying since the first questioning back at my house. At times, the prosecuting attorneys would even tell me that I was lying when, in fact, I was telling the truth. It had also been over two years since I had served as the Contracting Officer Representative—not the same as a contracting officer. The DOJ had copies of every email I had sent to or received from this contractor. They questioned me on the emails based on their interpretation of what the messages meant. I believe I was guilty in the eyes of the prosecutors before I was questioned the first time, and they were out to prove it.

It was incredibly exasperating, because I was enjoying my job very much at the time and felt honored to serve as the Chief of a team of subject matter experts; the best in their career fields. My position was authorized for the grade of Colonel, O-6 as the team leader. It was a very prestigious position—a job that I had wanted for almost fifteen years and took a great deal of pride in.

While on the team, we would actually memorize regulations and develop an inspection check list so that organizations could prepare for the inspections, and in turn, be as combat ready as possible. We would go out and attempt to find compliance or non-compliance to regulations, and then our report was written based on our findings—both good and bad. Soldiers whose areas were found exceptional were recognized during the out-briefing and presented with a team coin. This small gesture boosted the soldier's morale and inspired them to continue doing a good job.

My team was normally ten to twelve soldiers who over a three year cycle went to every state in the union, as well as Guam, Puerto Rico and the Virgin Islands. As previously stated, I loved the job, especially because of the travel, which was one of the reasons I had joined the military in the first place.

When I got the job in June of 2006, I really felt like I was on my way toward achieving what I had worked for over the past twenty-nine years. I had been thinking about retirement, but when asked to be chief of such a team, I couldn't possibly say no.

Things were going very well at that time. Even when General Petraeus was picked to go back to Iraq in 2007, he asked me to go with him and be part of his staff. I said yes, but little did I know what was in store for me and how my life would be changed.

During the ongoing questioning sessions, which even had me leave an inspection in Tennessee abruptly to meet with the DOJ, I did find a lawyer. A major who had worked for me and had unfortunately gone through a divorce knew of a lawyer who had been a JAG (judge advocate general) in the military. I hired him but did not retain his services for very long. At $250 an hour, and with meetings that would top the 4-hour mark, I knew this would be well beyond my budget. So, I terminated my first lawyer and sought out another after the first $7,500 was quickly expended. Through a contact given to me by another friend, I found a lawyer who I felt was competent and worked at a fixed rate. He was only affordable after I liquidated most of my retirement savings, but still more so than the first attorney.

I spent time with him explaining what had transpired thus far. I told him about the questionings, about Iraq and what I knew about the contractor in question.

My new lawyer accompanied me at the questioning sessions. He met with the prosecuting attorneys when we took bathroom breaks, and I was not privy to their discussions. I hoped that he could shed some light on what was going on, but in most cases he knew little more than I did, other than the investigation centered around one specific contractor in Iraq.

Contractors were in Iraq for a number of reasons. They would get jobs based on a need or a requirement that the military or the United States government could not otherwise fill.

They would identify a gap between capabilities and requirements to perform a given task, and then write a summary of the requirements to accomplish whatever needed to be done. The contractors would then be solicited for a company to perform the task. The need could be for anything from plumbers to supply clerks to transportation or security. Contracts could literally be on anything from A to Z. Whatever the need was, the contractor would try to fill it. In Iraq, the biggest needs I knew about were for security, transportation and logistics support. Contractors were in Iraq from all over the world, sensing the opportunity to make big money.

Once they got a contract, they would many times use workers from third world countries who they could pay pennies on the dollar, compared to American workers who wanted top dollar. The contractor in question was an American, and he had already gotten several contracts while in Kuwait and Iraq.

During the early questioning sessions, or interrogations, I was sure that it was the contractor they were after and did not see myself in any predicament. However, after one of these sessions, my attorney handed me several sheets of paper that had been typed up for me to read. I didn't understand most of it, which was in legal jargon, not to mention I became delusional during most of these sessions with the Department of Justice.

The section that pertained to me had mentioned conspiracy to bid rig and bribery. Until that moment, I did not know I was being charged with a crime. While I understood the word bribery, I did not know what conspiracy to bid rig meant, which I later learned meant fixing the bidding process on a contract to make sure one contractor was awarded the bid over another.

The two charges stemmed from two separate incidents, both of which had taken place after contracts were awarded. First, when I was leaving Iraq, I sold a trailer that I had been living in to this contractor in question for $4,000. This they considered to be a bribe. I was simply selling a trailer to whoever wanted to buy it. In fact, my lawyer told me that it would have been okay if I had sold it to anyone else. I only sold it to the contractor because he was willing to take it off my hands quickly, and I didn't want it being vandalized by the locals. More often than not, when Americans left belongings behind, they were vandalized or salvaged.

The other charge was that I took a vacation to Thailand after leaving Iraq. The DOJ claimed that it had cost $5,000 when it was really only $3,500. Regardless of the real value, I could not understand for the life of me how the DOJ could come to the conclusion that I had accepted a bribe of $9,000 after leaving Iraq to award a contract that had already been awarded months earlier. The reality is that $9,000 was not even a month's salary at my pay grade, which made the accusations more absurd. This did not even pass the common sense test. The bottom line and the truth is that there was never any agreement between me and the contractor for me to do anything for him in return for monetary or other gain.

I had been in Iraq working seven days a week, normally 18 hours a day for over the past two years, with short breaks every six to eight months. So when I left and was invited to go to Thailand before heading home, I never thought twice about accepting the invitation. I did think that I would be paying for my own ticket until the contractor dropped his wife and me off at the airport. He had already purchased tickets and refused to let me pay.

Quite frankly, I had no more fight left in me after the past year in the combat zone, experiencing combat fatigue and sleep deprivation. I was in a state of semiconsciousness from my lack of sleep over the previous 72 hours. So I innocently accepted the ticket, thinking it was in good faith for my support to his staff while in Iraq. At that time, all I really cared about was getting to a place where I could get some sleep.

As for the trailer, it was given to me by an Iraqi American in October 2004 who had fled the nation with his family. He had been working for the US government while living in Baghdad. However, someone was putting death threat notes on his door. Apparently, the terrorist had found out that he had been working with Americans, so they started threatening him and his family. He had a 6 x 8 trailer he had bought for the contractor, but it didn't meet his specifications. So the Iraqi-American gave the trailer to me, because at that time I had no place to stay and had been sleeping in my vehicle. I had worked with him before on various projects and knew him well enough that we had gained mutual respect.

Had the Army contractor provided me with a place to stay, which they were supposed to do, I never would have had the trailer in the first place. Management of living quarters had been contracted out to Kellogg, Brown & Root (KBR).

I had tried numerous times to get a place to live in contract quarters, but KBR kept telling me there were no vacancies. So, when I left Iraq, I thought nothing about selling the trailer. It just so happened that this particular contractor the DOJ was investigating bought it for $4,000.

Now it was all becoming clear. The Department of Justice wanted this contractor badly—for what, I was and still am not sure.

As my psychologist later explained, I was just a small fish caught up in a big net, and they wanted to bring me and, as I was told, 75 other people down in order to get this contractor. I'm sure there is a lot that I still do not know, but what I do know is that I never intended to commit a crime. In order for either of these acts to be considered bribery, they would have had to have been planned in advance of the bid, or at least this is what I had thought. They happened well after the bid was awarded, and there was no documentation of any advance planning for the trip or the sale of the trailer.

Cooperation to the Government

I was warned by the Department of the Army Judge Advocate Officers that I was expected to provide full cooperation to the government in regard to this case. The threat was that I would not only be prosecuted in a civil court, but I would also get a court martial if I did not fully cooperate. It soon became apparent that cooperation meant helping the government convict this contractor, and later giving a guilty plea. That said, I was told that I would be taking a trip to Kuwait to assist the government in obtaining more information related to the contractor in question. Wearing a wire did not affect me as much as the 3 CID Agents sitting two tables from me, listening to every word and movement made during my dinner. I had nothing to hide, but the sheer thought of being watched invades your territory, and the unknown of what they wanted me to say or do made me very uncomfortable. The thoughts of not knowing what they would do also made me nervous. The fact that I was told that I could tell a lie to gain information was very disturbing.

We ate at an Asia Hut outdoor restaurant behind my hotel (Hilton) in Kuwait City, Kuwait. The contractor met me in the lobby of the hotel, and we walked to the restaurant together with the CID agents trailing shortly behind, pretending to be window shoppers. After dinner, I had to report to their room in the Hilton to discuss the conversations the suspect contractor had made during our visit.

Now that I was cooperating with the Government, I thought things would get better. This was not the case; as soon as I returned from Kuwait the very next day, in fact, I was called into the Deputy Commanding General's (CG) office. The CG, Chief of Staff and Chaplin were waiting for my arrival.

The CG put a piece of paper in front of me to sign.

It was notification and acknowledgement of my Security Clearance being, as I recall, pulled immediately. During this meeting I was also informed that I would no longer be the Chief of the Command Logistics Review team. I was given a timeline to get my office cleared of personal belongings.

This meeting was very emotionally painful for me, as I cried through the entire meeting. My true identity had been taken away—a clearance I had held for almost 30 years, a job I had wanted for 15 years, and the respect of my subordinates, peers and superiors I had known and worked with. Although, those who knew me, and the values I held, have continued to support me. This is because those who truly know me also know I would never intentionally do anything immoral.

After this meeting, I was dismissed to report to the Chief of Staff's office to find out where I would be moved to in the building. I also lost parking privileges on government facilities and many times walked three blocks from my assigned duty station.

My first day in the storage room made me feel worthless; my access from the network had been taken, as well as the ability to call outside the building. I sat alone day after day for months with nothing to do. This is when I became suicidal and was put in the psychiatric ward at Bethesda Medical Center in Bethesda, MD.

When not being interrogated, I became paranoid that my every move was being monitored. The stalking from the reporters made a bad situation even worse. I never knew when or where they would show up. They even sat outside my residence hoping to get a statement. I managed to avoid them for the most part by driving out of my garage without stopping and directly into my garage when I returned home. I also would not open the door to the many doorbell rings from reporters. The questioning of my friends and other Army personnel did not start until after my plea of guilty to something I had never heard of. As a logistics officer, I knew very little about legal terms or contracting.

After my plea of guilty, the DOD IG (Department of Defense, Office of the Inspector General) started their own internal investigation to build a case for a court martial after the DOJ would be finished with me.

One of the Sergeants, who had worked for me and remains loyal, has his security clearance frozen. Their reasoning is that because he remains loyal to me, he is a suspect.

My life has been a day-to-day survival—very challenging. The VA doctors in mental health helped me survive by giving me excellent counseling and medication to calm my emotions and depression. At the time of this writing, my life has been totally miserable every day—all day, and every night—since this nightmare began on May 3, 2007.

I had finally been rewarded with a job I had wanted for 15 years. The first time I learned of the Colonel (0-6) slot was in 1993 when I served on this team as a Captain (0-3). I loved the job because I could build a team who worked together, enjoyed the job, and helped units (from companies to brigade level) to become more proficient and combat ready. The travel to a different state every trip, I also enjoyed; making positive changes to improve the compliance to regulations was a plus. I, along with my team had earned the respect of the logistics community by being knowledgeable, honest and firm, but fair. I expected the team members to fix deficiencies (if possible) before they left their inspection sites.

In contract, after the DOJ investigation on me started, I was labeled as a criminal and worthless, even before my guilty plea. I had no purpose other than to take up space and collect a check every two weeks, in which I did not feel I had earned. Yes, the DOJ investigation changed my life from having an extremely satisfying career to becoming a worthless individual.

Life Changed Quickly

What I never expected was how much my life would change. It was worse than a brutal divorce, and what once seemed so wonderful was now becoming a horrifying nightmare. When you are accused of a federal crime, you are helpless and at the mercy of the Department of Justice, and believe me, they have no mercy.

I remember saying at one point during the questioning, "If I'm such a bad person, why don't you just put me in jail and get it over with?" It didn't phase them at all. Nothing I said seemed to matter. In their eyes I was guilty, period. I thought you were innocent until proven guilty, but I felt that I was made guilty and trying to prove my innocence.

My attorney, in an effort to minimize the possibility of jail time and save my retirement, wanted me to plead guilty. I explained to him that I had no knowledge of any wrong doing. However, having taken the trip to Thailand and selling the trailer to this particular contractor were constituted criminal acts in the eyes of the DOJ, regardless of the lack of intent, and they were not going to back down from these charges.

My psychologist relates this situation to a friend asking

you to hold a bag for a moment, and the police suddenly arrest you because cocaine is in the bag. All of a sudden, you're in big trouble, and the police won't listen to the fact that you had no idea what you were holding. They'll simply arrest you no matter what you say, and they will presume you are guilty. The fact is that you were in possession of an illegal substance and now you must prove your innocence.

Perhaps the worst blow wasn't the accusations, because I still believed that I had not done anything wrong. The real twist on the truth came when the New York Times published a story in August of 2007 about the investigation based on pure speculation.

Until this article was published, no one knew of the questioning except my immediate chain of command, my attorney, the Criminal Investigation Command agents, and the prosecutors in the Department of Justice. My chain of command would not have told anyone, nor would my lawyer have divulged anything about the questioning. I believe the leak to the New York Times came from the Department of Justice, but why? It wasn't enough for them to destroy my life and my career; now I was further destroyed by the media.

The article entitled *Iraq Weapons Are a Focus of Criminal Investigations*, by James Glanz and Eric Schmidt, focused on federal agencies finding a widening network of criminal cases, which involved millions of dollars worth of weapons and supplies going to Iraq and being distributed. As stated in the article, it was comprised of "interviews with more than a dozen federal investigators, Congressional law enforcement and military officials, and specialists in contracting and logistics in Iraq and Washington who have direct knowledge of the inquiries." Here are some excerpts:

* * *

BAGHDAD, Aug. 27 – "One of the investigations involves a senior American officer who worked closely with Gen. David H. Petraeus in setting up the logistics operation to supply the Iraqi forces when General Petraeus was in charge of training and equipping those forces in 2004 and 2005.

"There is no indication that investigators have uncovered any wrongdoing by General Petraeus, the top commander in Iraq, who, through a spokesman, declined comment on any legal proceedings.

"Over the past year, inquiries by federal oversight agencies have found serious discrepancies in military records of where thousands of weapons intended for Iraqi security forces actually ended up. None of those agencies concluded that weapons found their way to insurgents or militias.

"In their public reports, those agencies did not raise the possibility of criminal wrongdoing, and General Petraeus has said that the imperativeness to provide weapons to Iraqi security forces was more important than maintaining impeccable records.

"'But now,' American officials said, 'part of the criminal investigation is focused on Lt. Col. Levonda Joey Selph, who reported directly to General Petraeus and worked closely with him in setting up the logistics operation for what were then the fledgling Iraqi security forces.'

"That operation moved everything from AK-47s, armored vehicles and plastic explosives, to boots and Army uniforms, according to officials who were involved in it.

"Her former colleagues recall Colonel Selph as a courageous officer who was willing to take substantial personal risks to carry out her mission and was unfailingly loyal to General Petraeus and his directives to move quickly in setting up the logistics operation.

"'She was kind of like the Pony Express of the Iraqi security forces,' said Victoria Wayne, who was then deputy director of logistics for the overall Iraqi reconstruction program.

"It is not clear exactly what Colonel Selph is being investigated for. Colonel Selph, reached by telephone twice on Monday, said she would speak to reporters later but did not answer further messages left for her."

* * *

When I asked what to do about reporters who started calling me, I was told by my attorney not to discuss anything with the press or return their calls.

The article went on to say that the Iraqi reconstruction program was estimated at $40 billion dollars. Also, according to the article, the Iraqi plans drew criticism for "Weak oversight, poor planning and seemingly endless security problems."

As I saw it, apparently by investigating and arresting everyone they could round up, the Department of Justice could find a way to put the blame on all of us who worked so hard over there, rather than on those who were not seeing to it that we were properly prepared and that there were systems in place to prevent corruption. It's easy to blame the little guy rather than take some overall responsibility, and that was what the DOJ was trying to do for the government.

The accusations against me were bad enough, but the worst part was how I was treated after the article appeared. The leadership where I worked took away my office, my Internet access and clearance.

I had been cleared for over twenty-eight years with as high as a Top Secret with Special Background Investigations. And now, I wasn't even allowed to park my car on the installation where I worked. I was basically relegated to a storage room and had no real responsibility. This was totally humiliating to me. After serving my country for so many years, I was being treated like a criminal, without a trial.

As a result of this humiliation, I tried to commit suicide twice and was hospitalized to keep me safe.

It was also around this time—an all-time low point in my life—that I learned how I became involved in this whole investigation.

I was told that a complaint letter was sent to the DOD IG from a guy whom I had fired in Iraq for not doing his job. This guy, JT, was supposed to be running a warehouse at the Baghdad Police Academy. He was supposed to be issuing equipment and uniforms to the new recruits who had already completed their training and were ready to go out onto the streets.

One time, when he was supposed to be doing his job,

he did not show up. I found out later that he was still in his trailer sleeping. As it turns out, a Master Sergeant, who was one of the Iraqi police trainers, went into the warehouse and found that nobody was there to hand out the uniforms and equipment, so he took over the job himself. At some point in the day, JT found out that the Master Sergeant was doing his job, so he came down to the warehouse to challenge this soldier. The Master Sergeant grabbed JT's arm and twisted it, resulting in his shoulder cuff being twisted out of place. As a result, I was called about the incident and told that I needed to conduct an investigation.

I then went to the Baghdad Police Academy Warehouse to question everyone involved and got sworn statements. This was not an easy task for a female traveling alone in the red zone from the Presidential Palace Green Zone to the Baghdad Police Academy, but it was sometimes necessary to get the job done. I found out that JT was slacking off more often than not. JT was frequently in his trailer sleeping and not supporting the operation. As a result, I had JT immediately removed from his position. It was him and another guy who then sent the letter to the DOD IG and told them I was involved in selling weapons to terrorists and that they were pretty sure General Petraeus knew about it.

While those accusations were obviously way off-base, they did draw me into the overall investigation of the contractor with whom I had been associated. It was the contractor who fired JT following my investigation of the Baghdad Police Academy warehouse operations.

The other guy, who I believe generated this letter, was the finance officer for the same contractor. When they initially got the contract, I was signing off on the vouchers so they could be paid for whatever work they had completed.

In the beginning, the first contract was for the establishment and management of five retail warehouses. There are various levels of the logistics operations, and the retail sites issue materials directly to the customers, which, in this case, were primarily the Iraqi Police, Border Patrol, and Facility Protective Service Officers.

The Facility Protective Services guarded key buildings and compounds, similar to what we sometimes call "rent-a-cops". They guarded museums, Ministry buildings and other key facilities that were identified as high-target locations.

We needed five retail locations established, each of which were supplying the Iraqi Security Forces with uniforms, weapons and other equipment. It took several months to get all five sites up and operational, so I pro-rated the contractor's pay to compensate only for work performed until all tasks in the statement of work were complete. I refused to pay for work that had not been performed in advance. So, as they got one warehouse up and running, I gave them a fifth of what they would have gotten if all five had been operational.

It took the contractor nearly six months to get all five warehouses up and operational. Considering the combat environment at that time, six months was acceptable and reasonable, and I believed no other contractor could have done any better under those conditions. Nothing was easy and everything took time with many setbacks due to terrorist attacks and damage from indirect fire. Apparently my decision to not authorize pay in advance didn't sit well with this particular finance officer, who joined JT to submit this letter to the DOD IG. Actually, it was an embarrassment to him when I told his boss the claims for payments were incorrect and needed to be corrected before I would make any authorizations.

Apparently, I did piss some people off in Iraq. If people didn't do their jobs, I was tough on them. However, you have to realize that you are in a situation where you've got staffers in a Green Zone protected by security. The combat fighters operating in the red zones were kids, mostly privates or sergeants, and if we weren't doing our jobs in secure areas, these soldiers could be killed or captured. At least that is how I saw it. I wouldn't tolerate incompetence or cowards not doing their job at the risk of our troops. I took my job very seriously, and if someone needed to be fired or if we had to prorate the pay to motivate people to do their jobs, then that is what I did to ensure the mission was completed and government resources were spent appropriately.

It was also around this time, during the months of questioning, that I learned about Gloria Davis. It seemed that after the investigation started, there was a Major who was a contracting officer in Kuwait. She had been working with the same contractor in question and apparently issued some contracts to him. Like me, she was questioned, interrogated and most likely was treated in the same manner—considered guilty from the start, prior to a trial. She admitted guilt, followed by her suicide. Whether Gloria Davis was really guilty or not, I do not know. I may never know what happened that would cause her to plead guilty or what drove her to suicide.

What I do know is that everyone who pleads guilty may not be. Like me, Davis (age 47) loved the Army. She was dedicated to the military and had served for 18 years. Like me, she had tried to commit suicide; the difference is that she succeeded. I don't think I ever met her, but I started wondering how many other officers would be brought to such a tragic end as a result of investigations and interrogations. From my experience, Army officers hold their positions in high regard. For a career officer to be humiliated and disgraced by the government in which they have served is horrendous.

A Cry for Medical Help

In October of 2007, the interrogation became more than I could handle, and that is when I became suicidal. I started seeing a psychologist, two actually. The first I was working with put me on convalescent leave for three months, which took me out of the humiliating situation of having to go to work each day, stay in a closet-sized room and not have a job. I had been in the hospital for nearly a month after my first suicide attempt. He did not want me going back to that environment where I felt useless and humiliated, so convalescent leave was a very good idea.

The psychologist I have now helped me realize that taking away my office and access to data wasn't personal and that it was just Army procedure that they must go through when someone is under an investigation. Still, I felt horrible and would stay awake most nights thinking about the whole ordeal. He prescribed medication to cope with everything and also helped me to compartmentalize, or put the situation in a file in the back of my brain, so I could function without allowing the tragedy to consume my every thought. Between the two psychologists, they have kept me alive and helped me get through it. If it wasn't for them, I'm sure I would have ended up just like Gloria Davis. I feel for her family. he should never have been pushed to the brink of suicide.

Fortunately, through all this time, I was still getting my military pay; however, I was not sure how long that would last. I had already spent a fortune on attorneys and had gone through most of my savings. I looked on the Internet and found out there is a law on the books from somewhere around 1965, stating that they can't take your military pay unless you do something that is a threat to national security.

Ironically, it was not that long ago when I felt so proud of my position on the inspection team and had visions of making my way up to Brigadier General. I continued to work hard with selfless service and total dedication to the county that I had served for over half of my life. Now, the only thing I could think of was to get out of the Army and try to save my military retirement. As I mentioned earlier, it felt like a cold and bitter divorce. You go from being in love and seeing a bright future to suddenly losing everything and feeling like all you want to do is run away from the situation and life.

Throwing in the Towel

In August of 2007, I applied for retirement from the military. My enthusiasm was gone, and all I felt like doing was calling it quits to a great love turned bad.

After seven months, in February of 2008, my retirement was approved, and I was out of the military June 1, 2008. The seven months of waiting seemed like a lifetime. Nonetheless, it was not the way I had envisioned ending my career, and while my military days were over, the investigation continued. It had now reached a point where my lawyer and I had to decide between the lesser of two evils since it was unlikely that I could convince the DOJ that I did nothing wrong—at least not planned or intentional. I was told that if I pleaded not guilty, I would be immediately put in jail, have to put up a bond and go through a trial. I was told that if the jury found me guilty, I would potentially lose my military pension, and that was something I simply would not risk. I could also end up in prison for a longer period of time and be fined a more significant amount of money.

I was told by my attorney that if I pleaded guilty, it would be considered cooperation with the government; my military pension would be at less risk, and I would receive a shorter sentence. I was also told the outcome is entirely the decision of the judge, but I would have to pay the $9,000 in restitution, which was received from the trip to Thailand and the selling of the trailer.

Tribune Wire Reports, June 11, 2008

"A retired Army Lieutenant Colonel pleaded guilty Tuesday to steering a Pentagon contract for warehouses in Iraq to a contractor in return for $4,000 cash and a $5,000 trip to Thailand.

"Livonia J. Sylph pleaded guilty to bribery and conspiracy in U.S. District Court as part of a plea bargain with the government in which she agreed to cooperate with the investigation. The Virginia resident also agreed to pay the government $9,000 in restitution and serve a prison term.

"She agreed to sentencing guidelines that could result in a prison term of up to two years and nine months. The length will be set by U.S. District Judge Reggie B. Walton on Oct. 14.

"The government said that in 2005 Lt. Col. Sylph of the Army National Guard served in Baghdad as head of a selection board that awarded an annual $12 million contract to build and operate Defense Department warehouses in Iraq. The winning contractor was not identified by name in the court documents."

This was the story as it ran in newspapers on June 11th, 2008. I made the newspapers world-wide when I pleaded guilty to something I was completely unaware was unlawful.

Plenty of other accusations started popping up, such as me fixing the bidding or lining up companies owned by the same contractor to make it appear as if there were other companies in the bidding process. Yes, he owned other companies, but the bids for the contract in question, to the best of my ability, were between other legitimate businesses. I did not know what this contractor's status or affiliation was in any of the other companies which he was involved, and did not know why I would need to know for that matter. I cannot fight the public opinion or what people decided to say in their blogs, although some people did defend me. Funny, when you plead guilty, some people want to stone you while others feel sorry for you … then there are those few—very few—who understand that when you're up against the DOJ, you may have no other recourse than a guilty plea.

The story of me pleading guilty was splashed all over the papers, and the media began hounding me. I would get phone calls filling up my answering machine tape, and, as previously stated, they would wait for me outside my home. They wanted to hear what I had to say, and I told them I had nothing. This went on for weeks until they got tired or my story was replaced by more important news. The truth was that anything they needed to know was available from the courts, or at least one side of this story was—my signed confession in particular.

I can honestly say that I knew all of what was written in the document I signed. I had been mentally and emotionally beaten down to the point where I would have signed just about anything or said anything they wanted me to just to make it all go away. My mental state was such that I could not concentrate or comprehend what I was reading. I cried and cried for hours on end day after day and night after night.

Of course, it still did not all go away, as I awaited sentencing. The trial for the contractor would also be coming up, or so I thought, and I believed that I would be called as a witness. How this would play out, and the effect, if any, this would have on my sentencing, I did not know. What I do know is that this is not justice.

In February 2008, an Iraqi who had worked as my translator for ten months in Tajo, Iraq came to the United States on a passport and lived in my house for almost a year. When I told him what had happened and was still happening with me and the Department of Justice, he said, "This is no different than Saddam."

What I did know was that the DOJ did all of this to get me to play ball on their team. It is for that reason that I decided to exercise my first amendment right of freedom of speech to tell my story.

I've cried more over these past three years than I had in my entire life. This has been a hellish time for me. Now, as I begin to tell my story, I can only wait to see how it turns out. Looking back, my desire to join the Army seems like it was in another lifetime. The 30-years serving in the military flew by faster, than the past several months. Admitting guilt was hard, especially when you believe you're doing so because you have no other way out, but waiting for punishment is also very hard. I've had letters sent to the judge on my behalf—letters that talk about my character and my accomplishments during my military career; one was even sent by General Petraeus himself. What I know from the bottom of my heart is that I served selflessly, proudly and honorably. Will all of my years of dedicated service and working round the clock to protect my country add up to anything? Right now, I can only hope so, because that, too, seems hopeless.

CHAPTER 2

A CHILDHOOD LONER

Chapter 2

A Childhood Loner

Living in Poverty

I grew up in a small town called Weiner in the Poinsett County area of Arkansas. The population when I was growing up, back in the 1960s, was roughly 500 people. As of the 2000 US Census, the town had grown to 760.

Jonesboro is the nearest city and home to Arkansas State University. As of 2005, according to the census, Jonesboro had over 59,000 people. It was also a much smaller city when I grew up.

My mom was one of 16 children (four stillborn), and my dad was one of 12. We were quite poor when I grew up. I remember going out to the fields with my dad, who was a farmhand, when I was about three or four years old, and by the time I was five, I was helping to earn wages by chopping cotton. My sister was six years older than me, and my brother five years older, and they were also helping out by working from an early age. My father instilled a strong work ethic in all of us, which certainly remained in me always.

I actually had another brother, whom I was closest to since we were only four years apart. He died when he was only eight years old. I missed him after his death and became somewhat of a loner since my two siblings were quite a bit older and didn't really include me in too many of their activities. Occasionally they invited me to join in, but I usually had to play the role of "Mikey", the kid on the old television commercials who became famous for eating anything, with his brother and friend always saying, "Let Mikey eat it."

Our nearest neighbors, about a quarter of a mile down the road, had two children who were about the same ages as my brother and sister, so they would all play together. They would set up a table made from boards across a bunch of bricks and make mud pies … then I would be the guinea pig who got to eat them. Other times, the two boys, my brother, and his buddy, would chase me around the yard with toad frogs and snakes. I guess it was typical behavior between brothers and sisters, especially those living way out in the country.

My brother was always getting in trouble. When I was about seven, my parents gave me a musical jewelry box for Christmas. We normally only got one gift and that was mine that year. Only a week after Christmas, my brother took it under the house and decided to take it apart to see what it was made of and how it worked. When my Dad found the pieces, my brother got into a heap of trouble.

Another time, my dad made us water guns out of wild cane pole. My brother was shooting cars that drove by our house with it, and again, he got into trouble. One time, my brother stirred up a bee hive of bees and they attacked me instead of him. My dad wore out the seat of his pants for that one.

Meanwhile, I was very sick and swollen all over. My dad went to the country store about six miles away and bought a watermelon for me, but I was so sick that I couldn't eat for two days.

My mom wasn't very involved in my childhood. She didn't seem to like me very much. I think she really didn't want to have more children, so when I was born, she left it up to my father to take care of me and basically had little to do with me unless it was to punish or abuse me. As an adult, my mother later on became my best friend, but as a child, my father took care of me and kept me away from my mom by taking me with him to the fields. Although, he was strict on all his children when it came to working and helping around the house.

One of the most pleasant memories I had growing up was going to church on Sundays and Wednesday nights. It was a very small Baptist church—no choir and nothing very fancy—but it was a place to be together as a family, worship our heavenly Father, and visit with our neighbors.

The preacher and his wife adored me and wanted to adopt me. I always sat on the preacher's lap at the church, and since my dad could not afford candy, the preacher would give me lemon cough drops. He told my parents that God had a special place in this world for me.

I remember one time my brothers, my sister and I actually did get candy. We went to the country store with my dad—the same one where he had bought the watermelon. Although far out in the country and on a gravel road, it was the closest store, in fact the only store for fifteen miles. It was a combination grocery store and supply store with a gas pump … kind of like Sam Drucker's store on the old television show *Green Acres*—selling a little bit of everything. I was about four, and my dad took us into the store where we all threw a fit for some licorice candy. Daddy told us we would not like it and that if he bought it we would have to eat every bite. We didn't really know what candy was and definitely had not heard of black licorice, but we sure wanted those licorice sticks since they looked very tasty.

Licorice was very popular at that time, and you could buy a dozen sticks for about a nickel, so we told my dad that the licorice was what we wanted. He wasn't happy buying the licorice, knowing we wouldn't like it, but he did it anyway, against his better judgment. And it is no wonder that when we got home, we grabbed the licorice sticks and started chewing away. We didn't know that licorice has an acquired taste, and since we were all pretty young, none of us liked it at all. In fact, we decided that we did not want to eat the rest of it. We also knew that our dad would give us a thrashing with a willow switch cut from the tree behind our house if he found us wasting his hard earned money. So, we decided to hide it in various places around the house, such as under the sink, between the mattresses, and in the back of the cabinets. Of course, after a few weeks we had completely forgotten where we had hid them, and every once in a while, pieces of licorice started showing up in all sorts of odd places around the house. It was very funny, but we could not let daddy see them, so we'd hide them again. To this day, I still remember this as a fun time I shared with my brother and sister.

Yes, we did have some fun times, but growing up poor, working throughout your entire childhood, and having a mom who rarely had much to do with you didn't make for the kind of childhood featured on most of the popular family sitcoms. Of course, until I got older, I didn't know that other kids had it any better. The more things you are exposed to when growing up, the easier it becomes to put your own life into perspective. Yet, I didn't feel sorry for myself; the more I learned about the world outside of my little corner, the more I wanted to get out there when I grew up.

Today, I look back at my childhood as a source of toughness and inner strength—qualities that would help me throughout my life—along with knowing what it means to work hard. My dad used to say the harder he worked the luckier he got.

My First Boots and Starting Grade School

The funny times; the silly things that happened along the way also served as a reminder that even though a lot of responsibility was thrust on my young shoulders, I did have some classic childhood moments. Probably one of the other funnier memories from childhood was from a time prior to attending school.

Both my closest brother and I were born with feet that were turned in somewhat, with the big toes pointing slightly toward each other. When I was three or four, the doctor told my parents that if we wore a special type of cast for a few months, since we were very young, the feet would grow straight. So, off we went to the doctor—my brother and I with my parents. We weren't quite sure what was going on, but my parents felt that this was important, and in the long run, they were right. So we drove off to Little Rock, the state capital, some two and a half hours away.

When we finally got there, we spent time with the doctor being fitted for these special casts. Like most kids, we did not want to wear them, so we did what any kids would have done in this situation … cried. As a result, my father, picking up on our dislike for our latest footwear, explained that these were actually boots. Being fairly young and unaware of exactly what was now on our feet, we went right along with it. Of course having cool new boots put everything into a different perspective. We had seen other kids with boots and knew that they were for wearing in rain and other bad weather. Boots could certainly withstand a tough workout. So, the next day, in the rain, my brother and I decided to test out our new boots. We proceeded down to a mud hole and began prancing around and playing; splashing around, jumping and doing all those things kids do that are both messy and fun at the same time.

When we were finally finished with our little escapade, we started walking home. However, our new "boots" didn't make the return journey as well as they had made the initial foray down to the mud hole. Instead, they started unraveling, much in the way a cast does when wet. Very confused at the sight of our new boots falling apart upon each step closer to home, we showed our parents what happened. Sure enough, a few days later, we were once again back in the car and driving two and a half hours for our second visit to Little Rock to get new boots—the kind that don't do very well in water. In the end, they did help to straighten our feet after a few months.

School was pretty far away, about ten miles, so we would take the bus every day. We didn't have much to eat for breakfast, and with older siblings, whatever we had was usually gone by the time I would try to get anything. As a result, I would go to school most days without breakfast. The school, however, provided a container of milk every day, even for those of us who could not afford to buy it. They also had a lunch program that gave those of us who were from poor homes a free lunch. Naturally, the school was divided into groups, or cliques. The richer kids hung out together and those of us who didn't have very much, hung out in our own groups. Until I was about seven, the schools were also segregated, so we did not have any black kids in our school until they started bussing them in as part of the law to desegregate the schools. Even though the government was trying to create racial harmony, it was not very popular among the people living in the South. Black and white kids did not have much to do with each other, nor did their parents. That was how it was in the South back then, and, unfortunately, it hasn't changed all that much today in many parts. My parents had black friends, so I was not raised to be racist, but it was the way many kids were raised in Arkansas in the 1960s.

I only had two dresses to wear to school, so I would wear one on Mondays and Tuesdays and the other one on Wednesdays, Thursdays and Fridays while my mom washed the first one. She would wash the other one over the weekend while I wore hand-me-downs or clothes that she would make for me, sometimes out of flour sacks. Not particularly attractive clothing, but something to wear

39

around the house, which was pretty far removed from any fashion critics; way out across the bayou in the country.

When I started school, I was pretty aggressive. I was a tomboy; pretty tough. I could outrun anybody in the school, including the boys. From all the work in the fields and around the house and defending myself against by older brother and sister, I guess I had a lot of energy. So, I spent free time at school running around and even wrestling with anyone who wanted to challenge me.

Since the school did not have enough buses for all the different routes, they would do a double run, which meant they would take some kids home and then come back and take the next bunch. So we would have to wait about an hour for the next bus to come back and take us home. There was one teacher who would watch us, but it was hard to keep track of all of us kids, so we could pretty much run loose all over the playground and around the little six room grade school. This is where I would get into wrestling matches, usually with the boys.

I was good at wrestling and would usually win. In fact, some of the kids would bring their allowance—I didn't get an allowance—which at that time was like a nickel a day, and bet on who would win the wrestling match. This went on for a while until I was twelve and starting to mature as a young girl. The boy I was wrestling hit me in the breast and it really hurt. I don't think he did it intentionally, but it was a wakeup call … Perhaps it was time to stop being a tomboy and start acting like a girl. So, at that point, my wrestling days were over.

Despite my tomboy years, I did notice boys, one in particular, Michael, whom I liked very much. He was really cute and appealing to my eye, and was the only guy who could beat me at tetherball. I found out that he liked me too.

I remember one time when we were in the third grade, Michael gave me a present. It was a ring—a diamond ring. Since I was still pretty young, I had no idea that a diamond was anything special, so I put it on and wore it home. As you might imagine, my mother was rather surprised to see her little girl wearing a diamond ring. She asked me where I got it and I told her that Michael had given it to me. That same evening, Michael's aunt noticed that her diamond ring was missing. After talking to Michael, she found out that he had given it to me. So the next day, I had to give back my rather expense gift. It was pretty funny, especially thinking back on it now.

I always got pretty good grades in school, which was very important to my dad who always stressed the importance of education. He told me that education is the one thing that nobody can ever take away from you. I have always remembered those words because they rang so true.

My dad worked for fifteen dollars a week, and I remember, even with that little amount of money, he still wanted me to be educated, so he bought a set of encyclopedias on a payment plan for $5 a month. I'll never forget his devotion to giving me an education, and I still have those encyclopedias even though they are obsolete.

I really enjoyed drawing when I wasn't at school or working. In fact, I was pretty good at it. I also liked writing poetry. It was a great way to express how I felt. I was still pretty young, and my writing skills were not that great. I would show my poems to my aunt, and she would mark them up as a teacher might do. It was something I was doing just for fun, but over the years, I lost interest because she was so critical. I never returned to either interest once I got older.

One thing I can say for my family is that we never had any drugs or alcohol around; we were too poor to afford such things. In fact, I don't even remember seeing meat on the table until I was about seven years old, and that was only because my uncle had a chicken farm and would give us chickens to eat. Many of the things people take for granted today were not part of life for us in the country farmlands in Arkansas. In fact, it was a very big deal when we were able to buy a television set in 1965, when I was in the fifth grade. There were only three channels that we could get, but I remember watching Wyatt Earp, Palladian, and some of the other westerns.

At that time, westerns were very popular. My dad would only let us watch shows that met his approval. He did not believe in space fiction or things that showed any form of violence, so we watched lots of westerns since they didn't really show too much violence. We also watched John Wayne and Clint Eastwood movies; since I was still pretty young, I also liked cartoons like Casper the Friendly Ghost. It wasn't like today where there are so many choices, so we couldn't be too choosy, but television was a nice way to spend the evening after school and work. I didn't have very much time for any kind of social life or after-school activities since I needed to pitch in and earn money for the family.

Growing up & Moving on

Middle school, known as Junior High School at the time, was totally uneventful.

In high school, I started dating. I was about 16 when I started going out with this guy named David who was a couple of years older than me. We would go to the movies or do other typical teenage things. Like most teenage boys, he wanted to get into my pants, but I wouldn't let him. The dating went on for a couple of months. I was under pretty strict rules about dating and coming home at a specific time, so when David brought me home late one night, my dad was not at all happy about it. In fact, he wouldn't let me see David again. I might have considered sneaking out to see him anyway, but my father was pretty tough, and getting him mad was not something I wanted to do. When I disobeyed, he'd slap me or give me more chores to do on top of my regular amount of work. I knew he was very protective of me and looked at me as the baby, even after I grew up. I felt bad, since David was my first puppy love and all, but I also believed I'd get over him with time. I got over him more quickly than I expected when he started driving around our road with another girl shortly after we broke up.

I didn't really understand why my dad had a different set of rules for me than for my sister. Perhaps the rules he had for me were stricter because of the mistakes my older sister had made. She got married at the age of fifteen with my parents consent. Why they had to give permission, at such a young age, I never could figure out. In those days, in Arkansas, the legal age for marriage was fourteen if you had parental consent, so fifteen wasn't that unusual for a girl to get married. In fact, if you weren't married by eighteen, you were considered an old maid.

Sissy's husband was a pleasant guy and really good looking—kind of looked like Bobby Darin. He would come over to our house and sit on the hood of his car and play guitar and sing. My sister fell for him hook, line, and sinker. I think he was her first love. Of course, I think she also wanted to get married to get out of the house. I don't remember exactly what the story was when she started dating; as to why my parents were okay with it. One reason I think they let her go out on dates was that one of my cousins was the same age as my sister, so they would go on double dates. That seemed okay with my parents. However, most things that Sissy did were okay with them, or so I thought.

When growing up, she was always my mom's favorite, and whatever she did was great … which was in stark contrast to the way she thought about me. It was a little like Cinderella, only I wasn't a stepsister or stepdaughter … I was her actual daughter, too, doing the chores while Sissy went off and got married.

Of course like many young marriages, it didn't end very well. While my sister was pregnant with her second child, she discovered that her husband was cheating on her.

They had moved to Hot Springs, which is a couple hundred miles away from Weiner. It's a small city, and they bought a house and rented out a spare room to a young woman for extra income.

One day, my sister came home early from work and caught her husband in bed with the other woman. That was the end of their marriage. She was clearly devastated and left him. I don't think she ever totally got over him either.

After my sister's marriage ended, she was still only eighteen years old, so she came back home and moved in, which was just fine with my mom.

When Sissy's second child was born, she let me name him, which was a great honor for me, so I chose the name Eddie Lee. My brother who had passed away when he was eight was named Edward, and now my nephew was named after him. Since my sister's middle name is Lee, I named him after my brother and sister. My Dad's name was already taken with David Ray, my sister's first child.

Since my sister did not appear very responsible at the time, I ended up raising Eddie Lee from the age of seven, while my mom was basically raising David Ray. Sissy was not a very good Mother back then. She was more interested in sowing her wild oats than taking care of her children, and I resented her for that. Here she had two beautiful children whom she couldn't take care of without my mom and I doing the job for her. She got married too young and now felt she had to make up for it by running around.

The next guy she spent most of her time dating was okay but nothing special. He wasn't particularly rich, but he would spend his last dime on my sister. I think that's what attracted her to him. She dated him for a while, and when they broke up, she went on to date other guys. While she wasn't much of a mom, I will give her credit for always working. She got a job as a waitress and a cook in a new restaurant that opened in our town. As I mentioned earlier, we all had a strong work ethic from our father.

When Eddie was a baby, I changed his diapers, fed him and looked after him a lot. I loved Eddie like he was my own son. We were always close, and he was the cutest baby I think I had ever seen. He was always a happy baby and pretty low maintenance. My parents also adored him. My dad felt that his grandsons were the greatest gift of his life, so he was very happy to have them around.

When I got older and moved out, my parents took care of both of my nephews until I joined the Air Force in 1978. I adopted Eddie when he was seven. My sister was not making very much money, and I could get him insurance and dental coverage from the military, so that seemed like the logical thing to do. Also, I was living alone, as I did for much of my life, and we really needed each other.

In Search of a Way Out of Poverty

I had moved out on my own after high school and gotten a job at a small dry cleaner. My life at the time was pretty uneventful. At one point, I switched jobs and went to work at the same restaurant where my sister worked. Making about $30 a day in tips was pretty good for the late 1970s in Arkansas—a pretty blue-collar state. Even though I was working and supporting myself, I didn't like the idea of always living from paycheck to paycheck, so I enrolled in a vocational school in 1976. Being that I didn't have much money, I was able to get a Pell Grant to go to the school. I studied office management, bookkeeping and clerical skills. After a year, I graduated and was awarded the most likely to succeed. Well, I certainly didn't succeed at first.

I moved to West Memphis, which is also in Arkansas. It was another small city located directly across the Mississippi River from Memphis, Tennessee, hence the name West Memphis. At the time, however, in the late 1970s, like most of the country, the area was in a recession, and jobs were hard to find. Despite my vocational training, I didn't have much work experience, so I ended up working at a 7-Eleven convenience store. It was at this point, in my early 20s, that I realized I had to do something different or I'd be in poverty for the rest of my life. I knew what it was like to be poor—I had grown up poor. I'd seen how hard my dad worked, but we could never get ahead. I decided that I needed to do something more with my life.

It was at this point that I first began thinking about joining the military. My father was against it. He was old fashioned and didn't think the military was any place for a young woman, but for me, it offered an opportunity to work and get a steady paycheck beyond the minimum wage. It also offered a chance to get an education and travel, which is something I always wanted to do. My parents had barely ever been outside of the state of Arkansas, but I knew there was much more out there, and I wanted to see more of the world.

Since I wasn't sure whether or not I would like being in the military, I first joined the National Guard. I went to a recruiter and was given a series of tests called the Armed Forces Vocational Aptitude Battery exam (AFVAB). In addition, you needed to have a high school diploma, which I had, and be in good physical condition, which I was. There are also height, weight and body fat percentage requirements, which I met, plus a drug test that I passed since I never did drugs. In fact, I saw one of those antidrug movies in high school about how drugs can destroy your brain, and it put the fear of God into me.

Very soon after the tests, I was accepted into the National Guard. Once you are in the guard, you normally report one weekend a month and for two weeks during the summer, unless you are called up for active duty. They also find a job for you, which for me turned out to be a finance specialist—maybe those bookkeeping courses did pay off after all. Essentially, the job meant keeping track of who attended drills, who should be paid and who should not.

I liked being in the National Guard very much, particularly the structure and the discipline. I was one of the few women assigned in the headquarters of a field artillery unit. Since I worked in the office with a desk job, none of the guys bothered me very much. For the first time, I had a sense that perhaps the military would give me a way to get out of a life of poverty and make something of myself. I was not adverse to hard work and began looking forward to moving to another branch of the military service. I was on my way to a successful and rewarding career.

CHAPTER 3

SIGNING UP TO THE MILITARY WAY OF LIFE

CHAPTER 3

SIGNING UP TO THE MILITARY WAY OF LIFE

My military career began in the National Guard, and it was a great experience. I was promoted from E-1 (Enlisted pay grade 1) to E-2 right after basic training. I was starting on a new road—one that would serve me well for most of my life. I made friends with one of my roommates, whom I would remain friends with for 30 more years. She's still in the Army, and like so many people who have known me for many years, she did not believe the stories she was reading about me. In fact, she knew I was not guilty and wrote a character reference letter to the judge on my behalf, along with some 35 other people whom I had known through my long military career.

From the National Guard, I moved on to the United States Air Force. I had talked to the Army recruiter, but he could not promise me a job right away. The Air Force, however, had co-ed basic training for women, which included a lot of domestic stuff at the time. I wasn't sure what my job was going to be since I enlisted with a general contract, but at least they were able to place me right away.

I was hoping I wasn't going to end up as a cook, since I didn't care much for cooking, but, being a risk taker, I was pretty much up for any challenge. After basic training, I was given three career choices—communications, dental assistant, or administration.

I was assigned to work in communications, as it turned out, where I learned how to operate everything—from a telephone switchboard to satellite communications. Switchboards were less sophisticated back in the later 1970s than they are today, with everything run by computers. You needed to know how to manually work the board and connect and disconnect calls. Satellite communications were rapidly evolving and would prove important as global technology continued to grow.

I also learned what is called cryptography, or "crypto", as it is known, which is a highly technical means of coding and decoding classified messages. Apparently I caught on quickly because I was assigned to work inside a vault and teach crypto to other enlisted personnel.

Of course one of the reasons I had selected a military career was to better my education, while another reason was to travel. Both of these goals were very soon realized.

While I learned the communications field, I was stationed at Tinker Air Force Base in Oklahoma City—one of many new cities which I would visit that I had never been to before. The base had opened just prior to World War II and repaired B-24 and B-17 bombers, while also fitting B-29s for combat throughout the war. Tinker had also kept planes flying through the Korean conflict, Vietnam War, and would later be used to support the troops, of which I was one, in the Gulf War.

It was there, in Oklahoma, that I also went to school at

night in an effort to get my associate degree. I was getting an education, traveling outside of Arkansas, where I had spent almost my entire pre-military life, and getting a decent paycheck all at the same time. As I saw it, life was pretty good.

One assignment took me overseas, and for six months, I found myself stationed on a classified mission in Cypress, one of the Greek Islands in the Mediterranean. Talk about travel; this was the farthest I had ever been from home sweet home Arkansas. It was actually quite an honor to be selected for this mission since only one other female had been chosen for this assignment.

Certainly the most beautiful part of the world I'd ever seen at that time, the Mediterranean had crystal clear water with rainbow colors and spectacular white sand beaches.

Working the night shift was perfect. I would go to work at 10 pm, get off work at 6 am, take a shower and go to sleep on the beach. By the end of the six month mission, I had a great tan.

When I returned to the States, I went to a six month school at Keesler Air Force Base, Mississippi and was qualified as an airborne communications specialist. I was assigned as a crew member on an EC-135 aircraft, flying twice a week between Peru, Indiana and Rickenbacker Air Force Base in Ohio. The acronym "EC" means the plane has electronics and cargo capability. This plane also performed airborne refueling missions.

There was significance to our missions, as a red phone to the White House was located onboard the plane. Of course I never used it, although it probably wouldn't have gotten me into as much trouble as the DOJ stirred up for me years later.

The one problem with this assignment was that I would get deathly sick whenever we flew, which, of course, was rather ironic for someone who had spent so much time in the Air Force. Of course, much of my first enlistment had been spent on the ground in vaults or participating in Joint Chiefs of Staff exercises with other military services.

One particular incident that heavily influenced my decision to go back to ground communications was a flight that I was on-board out of Griffiss Air Force Base (now closed). The EC-135 aircraft of which I was a crew member is a four engine plane. We lost one of our engines shortly after takeoff. This loss in itself was not a major concern. However, about an hour later, a second engine went out as we were flying at 30,000 feet over our orbit pattern in Virginia. The pilot decided the best thing to do was to terminate the mission and head back to the base in Indiana.

As we landed at Griffiss Air Force Base, a third engine caught on fire. Aware of our predicament, I remained pretty calm, determined not to panic. My boss, however, an E-6 (I was an E-5), was having a panic attack, and he was supposed to be in charge of the communication crew. The pilot had called ahead to Griffiss ground control to let them know of our situation and emphasized that we would be conducting an emergency landing. They were prepared, with fire trucks and rescue crews on the runway, for a less than smooth landing.

As we were cruising down the runway, one of the tires on the plane blew out and was also on fire. Now the entire left side of the plane was on fire. The pilot stopped the plane short of the mission control center, where the emergency vehicles were on the runway. We reacted quickly, performed an emergency exit as we had been trained to do, and everyone was then moved to safety. By then, the emergency crews were working to put out the fire.

I thought that perhaps this was a sign that I needed to find something else to do. I applied for a transfer and was moved to Griffiss Air Force Base in Rome, New York (also since closed) to work in a communications center. As soon as my enlistment with the Air Force was fulfilled, I moved back to Oklahoma City, Oklahoma and went into the Air Force Reserve as a cargo handler.

Joining the Officer Ranks

I was never one to just settle for the way things were at the time. I always wanted to move up and improve my position in life. That was true for getting out of a life of poverty, getting into the military and bettering my education.

My next goal was to get a commission, or in layman's terms, become an officer. The Air Force required a four year degree before you could apply for a commission. The Army, however, required a two-year degree. My obligation with the Air Force Reserve was near completion.

I continued to go to school at night and was working during the day. Initially, I was taking classes while stationed in Tinker, Oklahoma at Oscar Rose Junior College (now known as Rose State College). When I was re-assigned to Rome, New York, I transferred to Mohawk Community College, which is part of the State University of New York program. Along with my credits from Oscar Rose, Air Force Community College, and College of the Ozarks in Arkansas during my pre-Army days, I had more than enough credits to graduate with an Associate's Degree in General Studies.

I finished my Air Force Reserve obligation, moved to Phoenix, Arizona and enlisted once again in the Army National Guard. My first summer camp with the Arizona Army National Guard was two weeks of training at Fort Ord, California, a 28,000 acre fort built in Monterey County, about 80 miles south of San Francisco. The area was beautiful, and while it was tempting to go out and party with my fellow trainees as often as possible, I volunteered to do all sorts of details and extra duty instead. I guess that strong work ethic from my childhood was paying off; coupled with the fact that the only time I had tried alcohol, I got really sick, so I wasn't much of a party girl. I kept busy, and the two weeks flew by as I focused on my goal of getting a commission. I'd reached a point where I felt that if I wasn't able to move up to officer status, I probably would have left the military and utilized my communications skills to find a civilian job.

When I returned from Fort Ord, I had to take a test to find out if I could score high enough to be accepted into Officer Candidate School (OCS). I passed the tests and started OCS with the Arizona Military Academy.

Getting into Officer Candidate School was not easy, unless you compare it to getting out of OCS. Most schools encourage their students to succeed and want to have as many satisfied graduates and as few drop outs as possible. Officer Candidate School is quite the opposite. The tactical officer's primary objective is to try to get officer cadets to quit, which makes it extremely challenging. The idea is that you have to show extreme dedication and determination to get through the program, which is a combination of class work, drills and physical training. The classes are in areas such as leadership, military history, military customs and courtesy, responsibilities of an officer, codes of ethics and so on. Classes were difficult but nothing next to the physical training. If, for example, you wanted to eat lunch, you had to gain access to the mess hall, which had an entrance requirement—pull-ups. The pull-up bar was at the entrance, and depending on how long you had been in the school, you had to do from 5 in the beginning to 25 pull-ups at the end of OCS training before you could eat. Imagine if some of those fancy nightclubs with bouncers out front used such a requirement … they'd be far less crowded.

In this case, once inside, you then had to eat what is called in the Army "a square meal", which is best described as an old Army tradition regarding the way you sit in your chair while eating your meal. You are essentially forming a square with your upright, rigid body and then moving your arm (holding your utensil) in a square-like motion in order to get the food to your mouth. To top it off, you were only given about five minutes to eat, so the motions became precise and quick.

We also had numerous hikes with rocks in our rucksacks ranging from 10 to 60 pounds (which is half my weight). I recall having the flu during one five-mile hike while carrying 40 pounds of rocks. I did the unthinkable and got out of formation, which is something you simply never, ever do. I had a good reason, however … I had to throw up. The senior tactical officer saw me, came over to me on the ground and started kicking me.

When we returned to our barracks, he called me into his office and wanted me to sign a letter of resignation. He kept insisting, and I kept refusing to sign it. This too, was another test of your dedication and determination to be a leader. The Army does not want a quitter in a leadership position.

You could also be booted out of OCS if you got ten demerits (mistakes), and the tactical officers tried hard to catch you doing something wrong. At the same time, you try hard not to make mistakes.

As a cadet, I was continually put to the test. For example, we would be in class, and the officers would come into our barracks and ransack the place. Then, just like in the movies, we'd have to get everything cleaned up and put back in place before they returned for inspection. They only gave us about five minutes to put everything back together as best we could in that short time. The purpose was to build teamwork, because with only five minutes to put things back together, you would end up with someone else's mess kit, canteen, blankets and anything else you had on your bed display. You simply did not have time to worry about whose gear you were grabbing to get your display ready for inspection.

There were some things I liked about the OCS, such as marching in formation and calling cadence, which are the songs that we would march to. You would have to call the direction of march, and you did this by yelling "column left," or "column right," "rear march," and so on. The first word, such as "column" is called the preparatory command, and the last word, such as "right" is called the command of execution. If you weren't careful and paying close attention when calling cadence, you could walk the formation into a wall by saying column right when you should have said column left. When that happened, it was pretty funny.

The training was very intense at times. There was a lot of circuit training. We had eight different stations, and you had to do different exercises at each one. For example, at one station you would do sit-ups, at another it was push-ups; the next station may be running in place or jumping jacks and so on. It was like a smorgasbord of physically demanding activities, which the cadets had to do for an hour at a time almost every day.

Officer Candidate School at the Arizona Military Academy took a full year, and by the end of the year, the initial forty-seven officer cadets who started the training had dropped to twelve. I was one of the final twelve and in fact ranked as number two in my class. The Senior Tactical Officer said that no female would ever finish as number one in the class. There were three other female cadets who started the program with me, and we all finished. We stayed in touch over the years, and 30 years later, until my resignation, all were still in the Army. I was the only one who had been promoted to full Colonel.

When I graduated, the guest speaker was Arizona Senator, John McCain. He gave the famous "Duty, Honor, and Country" speech at the graduation ceremony. The speech was originally given in 1962 when Five Star General, Douglas Macarthur, accepted the Sylvanus Thayer Award and spoke before the corps of cadets at the United States Military Academy at West Point in New York. The speech talks about the responsibilities you accept as an officer, the duty you have and so on. It's a very moving and memorable speech that I tried to live up to throughout my career.

I was very proud to be getting a commission, and my family was beginning to accept my military career as they now recognized my achievements. I did feel bad that my dad, who was so instrumental in my life, was not around to see me make it as an officer in the United States Army.

Officer Basic Course

In 1986, I took the Officer Basic Course for the Adjutant General's Corp. It was in the winter at Ft. Benjamin Harrison, Indianapolis, Indiana. Not exactly like the beach in Cypress.

I had a roommate during my OBC named Jenny. She had long, curly blonde hair and had to get up thirty minutes before me every morning just to put her hair up since Army regulations forbid a female's hair to touch below the collar. I kept my hair cut short for the sake of saving time, plus it was easier to manage. Jenny kept me laughing with her continuous humorous stunts. She was also a Second Lieutenant during Officer Basic. Near the end of our training, we were required to go on a Field Training Exercise (FTX) to apply all that we had learned from the classroom. The training included application of reading a compass, land navigation, leadership, survival, first aid and so on.

We slept on the ground on a bed roll in sub-freezing temperatures in pup tents with two people to a tent. Luckily, my tent mate was a guy who learned from the boy scouts that sterno candles can keep you warm in cold temperatures, otherwise, I might have frozen to death. The leadership did not have to worry about anyone taking their clothes off; since it was so cold, the thought would never cross your mind. I slept in my clothes and normally had wet socks from patrolling or standing in a foxhole full of water. It rained or snowed every single day during our FTX and never got above 10 degrees Fahrenheit.

At night, after a day of land navigation, patrolling and wading through snow and mud, we all had a rotational two hour shift of pulling perimeter guard duty. We had to stand in foxholes full of ice-cold water up to our chests. We stood on wooden crates to overlook the deep foxhole full of ice water from the rain and snow.

On one of the patrols, the mission called for a wounded soldier, caused from direct enemy fire. Guess what—it was Jenny, the plumpest, weight controlled gal in the squad of five, who got the assignment. We had to treat her wounded leg and apply a splint. Then we had to carry her over five miles on a stretcher. We took turns carrying her because she was so heavy, and we were all getting tired quickly. However, we were determined to complete the mission as assigned. A form of teammate bonding occurs that is indescribable during these kinds of FTX exercises and other challenging times.

I experienced some great bonding in my 30-years in the military. It is these people who still know of my innocence who continue to support me and keep me going today.

The General—My Boss, My Friend

My first job after the OCS began in early 1987. I was

an administrative assistant to Brigadier General Robert Petticrew. Unlike some officers, he was a gentle man—kind, knowledgeable, and not at all intimidating. He was very highly respected by the soldiers and the community. It seemed to me that by the time some officers reached the position of General Officer, they left their disciplinary problems to somebody else.

I do recall that I was worried about his reaction to my first day of using a computer. At that time, computers did not have all the backup systems in place that many have today. So, within a very short time, I had accidentally wiped out the hard drive and lost all the files, which included plenty of data. This was not the impression I wanted to make on the General, so I decided to try to rectify the situation by staying up all night and trying to put all those records back into the computer—type in all the letters, etc. I was so scared that I didn't actually want to tell him what had happened, but I did, and he was pretty mild mannered about the whole thing, explaining that we had hard copy backups of the files, so there was no need to worry. Whew!

On one occasion he allowed me to go with him to the Western Aviation Training Site near Tucson, Arizona to conduct a staff visit. While we were there, he arranged for us to fly in the cobra helicopter. The cobra is a small reconnaissance, surveillance helicopter that can fly in very tight, unobservable places such as valleys and ravines.

When the pilot landed the cobra on the pickup pad, General Petticrew told me that I could go first. I thought that was a very gracious thing for him to do, since he was a general.

He sometimes brought baked pastries from home into the office for his staff. His wife was an excellent cook and we all gobbled up the pastries as if we were starving. He always cared for the welfare of the soldiers and periodically went to the armories to see how everyone was doing. During the time I worked for him as a Second Lieutenant Administrative Assistant, he became a father figure for me, treating me as one of his children.

When he found out that he had cancer, he decided to retire. Upon retirement, General Petticrew invited me to lunch at my favorite restaurant with him and his wife. They presented me with a silver platter that was engraved with: "To an Extraordinary, Dedicated Officer; General and Ms. Robert Petticrew."

When I gave his eulogy, the title was "A Soldier's Soldier." I sat up the majority of the night prior to his funeral getting the right words to say; how special he was to those who knew him. The words brought tears to even the toughest of the attendees.

Tough Duty

After General Petticrew retired, I worked for his replacement for several months, but he was not as personable or special as General Petticrew. So, I applied for another job in early 1988 and was hired as an Automotive Foreman in a Maintenance Shop where I would make more money.

I was mechanically inclined by nature, and growing up, my dad had taught me a lot about the different parts of a vehicle and how to repair or replace them. This was an opportunity to put that knowledge to use and to gain some leadership skills with 23 employees working under my supervision. It was also an opportunity to utilize what I had learned in getting my baccalaureate in business management.

I adjusted well to the position and had little trouble with my employees, with one exception. I had one employee, Pete, who had worked for the civil service for eight years. He had a zero sick leave balance, but still wanted to take off work to go to a doctor continually. After six months on the job, I refused to give him advance sick leave, and this is when the real problems began. He accrued two sick days every two weeks, and he took them as soon as they were accrued.

One day, my boss told me to drive by his house after he had taken off for sick leave, and sure enough, his car was sitting in the driveway.

I went back to my office and called the doctor from which he routinely brought in the doctor's slips after each of his many days off for sick leave. The receptionist told me that Pete had not been to their office for over six months. I explained that he was showing up with doctor's notes from the office for months, and even read off some of the dates of the notes. She told me that he must have stolen a pad of the pink slips that were pre-stamped with the doctor's signature.

The next day, sure enough, Pete came to work, and once again, he brought a sick slip from the same doctor.

I tried to suspend Pete for three days in accordance with union agreements, but he went to the labor relations officer who later called me into her office to discuss the problem. She told me that I should back off with the suspension; otherwise, Pete would have a heart attack. I refused to back off. The military sometimes has a way of either sweeping things under the rug or making a major case out of something small if they choose. So, I was moved by the Chief of Staff to another job with a promotion.

My new job was working as a Staff Officer, writing policy and tracking equipment readiness. I worked as a Maintenance Staff Officer from 1988 through 1993; with the exception of the time I went to my Officer's Advance Course in Ordnance (Maintenance Management) at Aberdeen Proving Grounds, Maryland in August of 1990; and when I was deployed into active duty for Desert Storm in December of 1990.

My boss was a colonel who was the toughest leader with attention to detail that I ever had during my career. As I look back, I am thankful that he was hard on me and had high expectations. I learned more from him than any boss I have ever had before or after.

As for Pete, his new boss was someone who never wanted to rock the boat, as is the case with many government workers. So, I can only assume that Pete just went on doing whatever he wanted to do. Although he might have had to find a new doctor—one who keeps all of his notepads under lock and key.

My Personal Life…

While Army life was good, marriage was not all it was cracked up to be. My husband and I divorced in 1989 after seven years of marriage. We had met in 1981 at a Christmas party. Our relationship was a no-no from the start since he was not only in the Air Force, but he was my commanding officer. I was a staff sergeant, and he was a colonel. We dated for less than a year and got married in Oklahoma City, where we were both stationed at the time. Knowing how difficult it would be for both of us to remain in the military, he decided to leave the service and went to work for Motorola. Once we were married, we moved to Arizona and settled in Chandler, near Phoenix. I actually got out of the military to go to school full time.

If there was such a thing as true love, I really did love that man … but within one year of our marriage, I realized that I couldn't trust him.

We had moved to Rome, New York at the time, and I was going to school nearby in Utica, where the college I was attending also had a campus. On this particular day, my newly-wed husband was supposed to go pick up my car at the garage. I'd had an accident a few days earlier, and it was being repaired.

It snowed so much that day; the school dismissed us early at about 2 o'clock, so I called to tell him that I'd go with him to pick up the car. His secretary, however, told me that he hadn't come in to work that day. I called the office a few more times, and still no sign of Jim. I thought perhaps he was sick, so I called the house … still no sign of Jim. At this point, I began to think something was definitely wrong, so I drove over to the garage and waited to see if he ever showed up. I sat in my car for roughly two hours before I saw him and a woman show up to get the car. They drove off, and I followed them. Within a few miles, they pulled into a hotel parking lot. My anger was building, but I stayed back and watched and waited. Sure enough, they went to a room. That was it, my blood was boiling, and I'd caught him in the act of deceit. I headed for the room and knocked on the door. Needless to say, he was very surprised to see me! "What the hell is going on?" That was my first and only question as we proceeded into a fight that didn't last very long because I took off in an emotionally painful rage. I went home and locked all the doors and windows. We'd been married less than a year, and I couldn't believe he would do this to me.

A short time later, he came home but could not get in as the doors remained locked. He shouted for me to let him in, but I had no intention of doing any such thing. Finally, he broke a glass window in the kitchen and got into the house. There I stood, holding a gun pointed in his direction. I warned him that if he ever slept around with another woman again while we were married, I would kill him.

I never totally trusted him after that. You can never go back. We did get past it and stayed married for six more years. I've kept his name, Selph, to this day. We had good times, but things changed over the years, and the trust diminished to ground zero.

By the time we separated, we were sleeping in separate rooms. He wanted me to get out of the Army, which was a major time commitment and the most important part of my life now. I was married to the Army, and I did not want to leave. He gave me an ultimatum. I still did not want to leave the Army. I never thought he'd actually go through with a divorce, but he did. I had been on my own for years, so it wasn't too hard to adjust to being single again. I was hurt but moved on with my life and my career.

Jim, meanwhile, got married again six months after our divorce. Looking back, even the pain of him cheating on me and the divorce did not compare to the betrayal and pain recently inflicted on me by the United States Military and the DOJ.

CHAPTER 4

OPERATION DESERT STORM

CHAPTER 4

OPERATION DESERT STORM

As a part-time soldier in the Arizona Army National Guard, I was assigned as a Platoon Leader in a transportation company in 1987. It was a fun job, and I enjoyed it very much. I also enjoyed working with the soldiers and seeing results from our work. Most of the soldiers enjoyed working with their comrades and the resulting teamwork.

I was promoted to first lieutenant in 1988. I felt a sense of accomplishment from my hard work and just wanted more of what I enjoyed—"Duty, Honor, Country." I prided myself in trying to be the best at everything I did as an officer.

I worked as a maintenance manager until August of 1990, as previously stated, when I attended my Officer Advance Course in Aberdeen, Maryland. I had also started working for my graduate degree in adult education, but took a break from college while I attended my career course. I purchased a new camper trailer and lived in it at a local RV camp ground to save money while at Aberdeen.

The Officer Advance Course was extremely tough, and

I had to study very hard every night after a day of classroom instruction. Many nights, I would not finish studies until 0200 hours in the morning.

During the first week of our course, the deputy commander addressed my class. He made it very clear that he did not care if anyone graduated and that we would not graduate if we did not study. He was a one star general who enjoyed running with the students at the Ordnance Center and School. God forbid if you did not stay with the formation and finish these fast paced runs.

Later on, I learned that this particular general had a heart attack and died right outside the gym after a run in Seoul, Korea. It is not unusual to see soldiers and leaders in the Army pushing themselves to the limit, and I was as guilty of this as anyone that I have ever known. Fortunately, I had better results than the General.

My Officer Advance class was scheduled to graduate the second week of December, 1990. The troop ramp up for operation Desert Storm had started earlier that year in the form of Desert Shield. There was a significant shortage of transportation officers in the Middle East at that time, so I was asked if I would volunteer to go to the Gulf. I responded that I would volunteer to go and serve my country.

As a result of my decision, I was allowed to test out and graduate a week early to depart for my mobilization station at Fort Huachuca, Arizona. From there, I would leave for the Middle East. At this point, having been so engrossed in the Officer Advance training, I had little time to follow what was going on in Kuwait. I had no time to watch the news reports on television, so I only knew the basics—that there was a conflict and that United States troops were being sent over in an effort to support an allied nation.

I drove non-stop from Aberdeen, Maryland to Memphis, Tennessee in the rain and snow with my camper trailer in tow. I planned a layover at my mom's, which I thought was about half way to Fort Huachuca.

I was within 50 miles of my Mom's house in Northeast Arkansas, the trailer slid on the ice and jackknifed into the side of my Bronco. This was before I had a cell phone, so there I was, stuck in a ditch with the trailer against the side of my truck. One of the locals saw what happened and stopped to offer help. I asked him to call my Mom's house and tell her what happened, where I was, and to send my two nephews to help me.

After sitting in the cold for about an hour, my nephews showed up to my rescue. They pulled me out of the ditch, and one of them drove me to my Mom's house. It was between midnight and 0100 hours when we got settled. I was exhausted! I asked my Mom to wake me at 0600 hours, which she did. I was back on the road by 0630 hours. I drove non-stop to Albuquerque, New Mexico, where I stopped because I could go no further.

I called a friend in Phoenix, Arizona and asked for help. He flew to Albuquerque, where I picked him up at the airport. He drove me the rest of the way to Fort Huachuca, Arizona. At that point, I was suffering from physical exhaustion and was diagnosed with mononucleosis then put on bed rest for two weeks. That is when I realized that very few people care about how hard you work, and that when you are down, life goes on for everyone else.

For two weeks, while I was on bed rest, I did not get a single visitor. By mid-January 1991, I was up and about again and into mobilization training to prepare for deployment to Southwest Asia.

The Face of War on the Horizon

During the summer of 1990, long standing tensions between Iraq and Kuwait had resulted with the Iraqi President, Saddam Hussein, amassing troops along the Kuwaiti border. While Saddam Hussein had promised more negotiations before invading Kuwait, these negotiations did not occur, and in August, the Gulf War had begun as Iraqi troops invaded Kuwait.

There were immediate economic sanctions imposed on Iraq by the United Nations Security Council, but there was also preparation for outside forces to get involved in the conflict—not only the United States, but Great Britain and nearly a dozen other nations. Operation Desert Shield was already underway, with U.S. troops already deployed in Saudi Arabia to prevent Iraq from invading into that nation.

Battleships such as the USS Missouri and USS Wisconsin were sent to the area to help build up the military shield and line of defense. The buildup, mostly from the United States, would eventually total more than half a million troops, which I would soon join.

We were shipped out of Tucson, Arizona on United Airlines with a civilian crew. They treated us very well and even exchanged names for us to write and stay in contact with while we were in the Persian Gulf.

It was a long flight. When we finally landed at King Fahid Airport in Saudi Arabia, all of the officers except me got off the plane. I had learned in OCS that you don't go before your soldiers; you don't eat before they eat, and you make sure they are taken care of before you take care of yourself. This was ingrained in me, so I waited for my soldiers, some of whom had started unloading the plane, when the military police came on the plane and told us we were under a "red alert" and that we had to close the plane doors and take off immediately. With a few of the soldiers and me on board, the crew took off unsure of where or when we would be able to land.

We made numerous attempts to land that night, and we were fired upon by Scud missiles each time. I assured the crew and the soldiers that we were only in an exercise and we were testing "touch and goes."

We did touch and go exercises quite often while I was on flying status with the Air Force in the early 1980's. Each time we would try to land, we would take off again until we were forced to land for fuel at approximately 0400 hours. We stayed on the ground just long enough to get fuel, and then were back in flight. I, nor the soldiers, knew where we were, and at this point, we realized this was not just an exercise. The Iraqi military was firing at us and were trying to kill us.

As it turned out, on that night, January 17, 1991, the President of the United States, George Bush (Senior) declared war, and we were under fire the entire night. Finally, at 0800 hours in the morning on the 18th of January 1991, our United Airlines flight landed at King Fahid Airport where we all disembarked to find the commander of my unit along with all the other soldiers who had not been flying around over the skies of Saudi Arabia. We were relieved to see them. Operation Desert Shield had now become Operation Desert Storm.

When we arrived, there were thousands of soldiers at King Fahid Airport who had been there for days, unable to leave. The problem was that combat troops were being brought in much faster than they could be transported out of the airport. They didn't have enough transportation or logistical support to get them out of the bottleneck. As a result, all of the portable johns were overflowing, and there was human waste everywhere. Many of these soldiers had not eaten for days, nor had they had water. It was really a personnel jam-up without logistics support.

We had brought along three pallets of Meals Ready to Eat (MREs) and three pallets of water to hold the company over until we were settled at our field base. As soon as I saw the conditions these soldiers were living in, I wanted to give them some of our MREs and water. My Commander refused, and he and I did not get off to a good start. He thought only about his own company, while I, on the other hand, saw a soldier as a soldier, and we should all stick together during war (or so I thought). Because he out-ranked me and was my commanding officer, I lost that battle.

Rumor has it that one of the soldiers who had been there for several days had a father who was a U.S. Senator. The soldier was able to contact his father, and when he did, all hell broke loose. The problem was rapidly fixed to say the least.

We stayed overnight at King Fahid Airport and were then bussed to the Port of Dammam on the 20th of January.

For the first couple of nights, we stayed at the Kobar Towers, a high rise apartment complex. The apartments weren't furnished, but we were so tired that we really didn't care that we had to sleep on the floor. We just needed a place to stay until we were ready to move into the desert.

All night and early mornings, the Iraqis were firing Scud missiles at the Kobar Towers compound in which we were staying. The Scuds were not very accurate and did not often hit their targets. My company was on the third floor. The first night, we had to sleep in our MOPP suits and with our masks on because we didn't know, at that time, whether the Scuds had chemical loads or not.

I recall waking up the next morning and going downstairs. I had taken my mask off, wanting to get some fresh air. Then we heard a Scud coming, and I remember running up those three flights of stairs faster than I'd ever climbed before, moving four steps at a time. I put my mask on and didn't take if off again until we started moving forward into the desert.

After two nights in the Kobar Towers, at around 2100 hours, the commander directed me to go forward and set up a base camp near our parent battalion. A Sergeant from our parent Battalion had come to the port to escort us to the location where we were to establish base operations. The only soldiers I were allowed to take along were the cooks and one supply sergeant.

As we left the Port of Dammam, I saw a stiff body lying on the side of the road and could not imagine what could have happened to this man. The image of this body stayed on my mind for several days.

We drove on a major highway for about three hours, and then we drove around in the pitch-dark desert for hours and hours. I did not know where we were going or how far it was to the battalion, so I didn't know that the sergeant had gotten us lost in the middle of the desert. We had to move with lights off in the pitch-dark desert with a very hard rain coming down, so it was understandable that anyone could get lost.

The next morning, we found our way to the battalion. It was still raining very heavily. The sergeant dropped off the soldiers and me along with two flatbed trailers loaded with twenty foot container boxes.

The container boxes were loaded with tents, tent liners, tent poles, stakes, and ropes for building our base camp. We quickly discovered that the containers were placed door to door, facing each other on the flatbed trailers with only about 18 inches between them. Normally, there were cranes to unload these massive boxes filled with equipment and supplies—not unlike the boxes you would find on a railroad freight train. The supply sergeant managed to squeeze through one of the container box doors, just enough to get inside and pull out the tent pieces one by one. We got enough parts out of the container box to set up two tents. This task took us a good part of the day, and until we were finished moving the equipment piece by piece, I was so angry that I could have chewed nails.

I quickly discovered that the cooks were helpless when it came to putting up a tent and did not know much of anything beyond cooking. I knew how to put up a tent from my Air Force Mobile Communications days, and the supply sergeant also knew how to put up a tent. However, none of the nine cooks had ever been trained to perform that simple task.

By night, we were all exhausted. The supply sergeant and I had put up a twenty-man tent with no help, and I was so mad at the cooks that I ordered the nine of them to put up the other tent. They put the canvas on the inside and the liner on the outside, and I made them sleep in it until the remainder of the company arrived at about 2230 hours that night.

It was cold and still raining. We only had our bed rolls that were wet and cold. The Commander, on the other hand was so upset with me because I had not completed the base camp, that he made me and the other soldiers put up another four tents that night. Needless to say, we did not get any more sleep that night.

The next day, the commander sent the other Lieutenant in to the battalion to borrow a forklift and a crane to offload all the containers from the flatbed trailers. We completed establishing our base camp the second day in the desert and were the only organization in our base perimeter.

Over the following two days, we built a perimeter defensive wall with a backhoe and concertina wire on top. We dug fox holes for security watch in the walls of the dirt perimeter to see any and all approaching vehicles. We had one way in and one way out with a security guard post.

Our battalion was set up one mile away from our base camp. Every day at 1700 hours, all the officers in the Supply and Services Battalion met for a Command staff meeting, where we would report our accomplishments to the commander and get mission orders for the next day.

I shared a tent with another female Lieutenant who did not know how to start a fire in our potbelly stove to keep our two person tent warm. Since we were in a petroleum truck company, we were never without fuel. We mixed our fuel with 50% mogas (short for motor gasoline and used as aviation fuel) and 50% diesel for our little stove. The mixture sometimes got so hot that the side of the stove was candy-apple red, but it sure did keep our tent toasty.

One night, I was having trouble starting the fire. After putting about five matches in the stove belly, with no luck, I raised the lid to look inside just as the stove blew up in my face, and I was burned severely. There was nothing I could do about it but wait until the pain went away and give it time to heal.

At the next staff meeting, the battalion commander asked me what had happened to my face. Light heartedly, I told him that I was attacked by our pot belly stove and asked if I could get a Purple Heart. His response was, "Only if the stove looks as bad as you do." That gave the entire staff a chuckle, including me.

Grubby Days at War

After two weeks in the desert without water for showers or any way to wash our hair, I decided to get my hair cut. We did not know when we would be getting shower water, so it seemed like the most logical thing to do. I went into the supply tent where the company barber cut the soldiers' hair at night. I saw that the scalp of the soldier in the barber chair was full of sores. It looked terrible and very unsanitary. I got in the chair when my turn came and told the barber to cut my hair off to the scalp.

He said, "Are you sure?"

I said, "Yes," and before I knew it, I was as bald as any of the guys.

The following week, we were directed to purge two of the diesel tankers to haul shower water. We built field showers out of plywood and hauled water in our diesel tankers from a locally discovered water source.

Everything seemed to be fairly uneventful while we just hauled fuel and water for the next several weeks as our primary mission. The commander would not allow a convoy to move unless a lieutenant was accompanying the mission. There were only two lieutenants, so we stayed very busy. We were only hauling diesel and mogas until after the ground war. We were hauling fuel to all geographical areas in Saudi Arabia and Kuwait.

On February 20, 1991, we started the plans at the company level for the ground war. We got our orders to stage for the attack on February 22, 1991. We staged at what was known as the Dust Bowl, and it was called this for a reason. The desert was very dry, and there was plenty of dust anywhere a vehicle moved.

We staged behind the Third Armor Division. There were Bradley tanks as far north, east and west as the eye could see. When the tanks took off at approximately 1600 hours on the 23rd of February, the entire sky was full of thick dust. Visibility was null. What made it worse was that Saddam Hussein had his troops set fires to the oil fields, and the black smoke from the fires made it even more difficult to see anything.

Approximately 3 hours after the tanks departed the Dust Bowl on the Green Line, the tanker trucks, which were 7.5 ton supply trucks, followed traveling north. I was in one of the platoon leaders' trucks, which was a camouflaged SUV that rode like a buckwagon. All the vehicles were marked with a large "V" painted black on the doors and roof of each vehicle. These markings were to ensure friendly fire was not accidently turned on coalition vehicles. My company drove with the battalion lead until approximately 2200 hours on the 23rd of February. We had a rendezvous point south of the Breach of Iraq with a scheduled hook-up time with the armor, (a.k.a. the tanks). Although we did have GPS systems that gave the longitude and latitude at that time, it was still very hard to know where you were going in the dark of the desert. We might have crossed into Iran at some point in our travels but really didn't know for sure how far north we had travelled

After driving for several hours in the dark to our planned hook-up location and time, there were no tanks. We sat in the middle of the desert for several hours until the battalion commander found out why the tanks had not connected with us for a refueling. He sent a couple of officers forward across the breach to find the tanks. The officers returned around 0400 hours in the morning, and from there, some of the fuel trucks were ordered to move forward onto the battle field, and the remainder of the battalion was ordered to unload and build a bag farm in the desert.

A bag farm is made up of huge rubber bags that hold about 50,000 pounds of water or fuel. It's a mini service station of sorts where the tanks and helicopters could fill up in the middle by bag.

I was ordered to return to our base camp in Saudi Arabia. The supply tent had caught fire and burned with all of our supplies and several M-16 rifles. I went back to the camp and did a report for our commander. The ground war only lasted three days, and by February 26th, the Republican Army was waving white flags in surrender.

After the ground war, my company began hauling everything that a tractor truck could hook on to. We hauled water, mail, food supplies, fuel, concertina wire, plywood, you name it. I was sent on a mission to resupply a Brigade of the Third Armor Division, which was holding ground in Kuwait. I took twenty trucks with supplies on the 15-hour convoy.

En route, we encountered a couple of challenges. We had to drive through the smoke from the oil fields that were still burning in Kuwait. The trucks were moving along bumper-to-bumper with only cat-eye lights. We also had to cross a field of grenades at night. To make sure the trucks did not hit a grenade and cause a massive explosion, I walked in front of the lead vehicle of the convoy and cleared the mine field very carefully with my bare hands. I knew what had to be done. I knew I was at risk and so were my soldiers. If one single grenade had blown, the oil tankers would have exploded with a disaster that could have killed many thousands of people. I was using a flashlight to find grenades on the dirt road and moving them to the side so the trucks could get through safely. I was scared and sweating bullets as I proceeded extremely carefully. The convoy safely moved through the mine field at a snail's pace.

We got through the obstacles and reached a brigade of the Armor Division where we delivered the supplies. The commander was a colonel who needed the haul capability that the tractor trailers provided.

After we unloaded the supplies, the colonel ordered me to stand fast and not return to my base camp. I called my own commander who was a major at that time. The major ordered me to return immediately to our company base camp to support other missions. As a lieutenant, it put me in a pickle, and, receiving two conflicting orders from two superior officers, I did not know what to do. I decided to follow the orders of the colonel since he was the higher-ranking officer, and he was giving me a direct order.

My company commander was not a happy camper when I got back to our base camp four days later, after the colonel finally released my platoon of trucks and soldiers. In fact, he ripped into me like I was a private when I got back to our base camp. Although, today, as I look back, I believe that I did the right thing by obeying the colonel's orders.

In the aftermath of the war, while taking care of refugees, and during the Medallion of May 1991—a military event—the company in which I was assigned got orders to return to the States. Twelve soldiers were ordered to stay behind and support humanitarian missions. I was asked to stay behind with them, and I did just that. The soldiers were not very happy. Everyone was anxious to get back home to their families, so I was privileged to work with twelve disgruntled soldiers. Many of them assigned to the humanitarian mission went AWOL, going to the airport and seaport in attempts to get back home any way that they could. As a result, the Military Police set up checkpoints where soldiers could not get through unless authorized.

General Franks was in charge of the humanitarian missions, and was very aware of the problem. He called a staff meeting with the hand full of officers left behind and told us to go back and tell the soldiers that they would all get a "Humanitarian Service Medal" for staying behind to help support the Refugee Camps. I went back and gave my soldiers the general's message, and their response was simply, "Tell the general to stick his 'Humanitarian Service Medal' where the sun doesn't shine." The soldiers were still very unhappy, but did their job regardless.

We completed the humanitarian mission of hauling food and water to the refugees—to people who hadn't had anything to eat or drink in a long time—in July 1991. When we first brought the supplies in, there was fighting over the food and water, so some MPs came and fired shots in the air to get everyone's attention and to try and restore some order. This allowed us to hand out the food and water to make sure everyone got some. The refugee camp was in the middle of the desert with wire around it. The refugees slept on the ground in bed rolls. By the time we left, the people were sent back to their homes, as the war was over.

After working until completion of the humanitarian mission, I was once again staying in Kobar Towers, this time for several months. Not long after I returned to the States, Kobar Towers was hit by Iraqi missiles, well after the war. Several American Marines were killed in the attack, yet the United States did not retaliate.

It was also after the war that I did get to see Kuwait City, which is a fairly developed city with stores and pretty much anything you would want to buy, much like a United States city, although the quality of goods was not at the same standards; the city and most of Kuwait was still recovering from the war. While it wasn't written about in most of the newspapers, there was a third part to the mission. Following Desert Shield and Desert Storm, we had Desert Fix, where we worked to restore the desert area and the terrain to what it was before the fighting and the many fires.

At this point, we were then sent to the Port of Dammam to load ships with equipment that had been left behind. We had to wash a lot of equipment and have health inspections to make sure things were not contaminated before we could put it on the ships to send back to the States. The mission was completed in September 1991, and we were finally released to return to Fort Huachuca, Arizona.

When I returned, I received a Humanitarian Service Medal. I felt good about myself, knowing that I had performed my duty and did what was expected of me in a difficult situation.

After completing the demobilization processing, I returned to Phoenix, Arizona to my staff job in logistics. I continued this job and went to night school, once again working toward my Graduate Degree in Adult Education. It didn't take me long to feel comfortable back in school since I had been in so many classrooms before the war.

It had been suggested to me, several years earlier, that I pursue a degree in education in case I wanted to teach when I left the Army. Although a friend, who had been teaching for a while, told me he didn't think I'd like it very much, I completed my Master's Degree nonetheless. I knew that if I wanted to be competitive in the job market after leaving the Army or retiring, it was important to have a Master's Degree.

At this point, I was assigned as a Battalion S-4 Logistics Officer as my weekend job, and then promoted to Captain in June 1993. I then took a job in October 1993 on Active

Duty with the Active Guard and Reserve (AGR) as a Branch Chief over the Maintenance Management Inspection Team. This was a great job that I enjoyed very much. My career in the Army was, at this time, going very well.

Figure 1: Hodgee Market before bombing.

Figure 2: Aftermath of the bombing in the Hodgee Market where I and other soldiers shopped for Iraqi goods.

Figure 3: Iraq Car Bomb—April 2005—Aftermath of a roadside bombing from an IED. The mirror you see is of the vehicle that I was in.

Figure 4: The little Iraqi town that John Hess and I traveled through to escape a "hot" zone where a bomb had just gone off.

Figure 5: One of Saddam's palaces at Camp Victory, near Baghdad International Airport.

Figure 6: Sandbag security perimeter around the trailers in which we lived in the Green Zone.

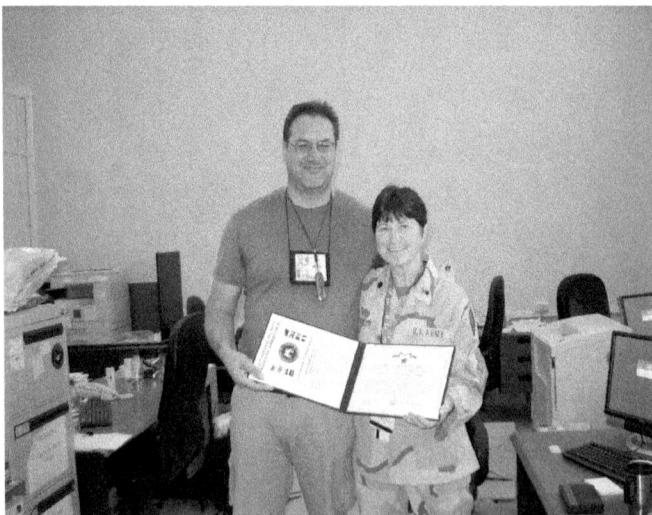

Figure 7: John Hess taking a photo with me after I received my first bronze star.

Figure 8: BPA Weapons

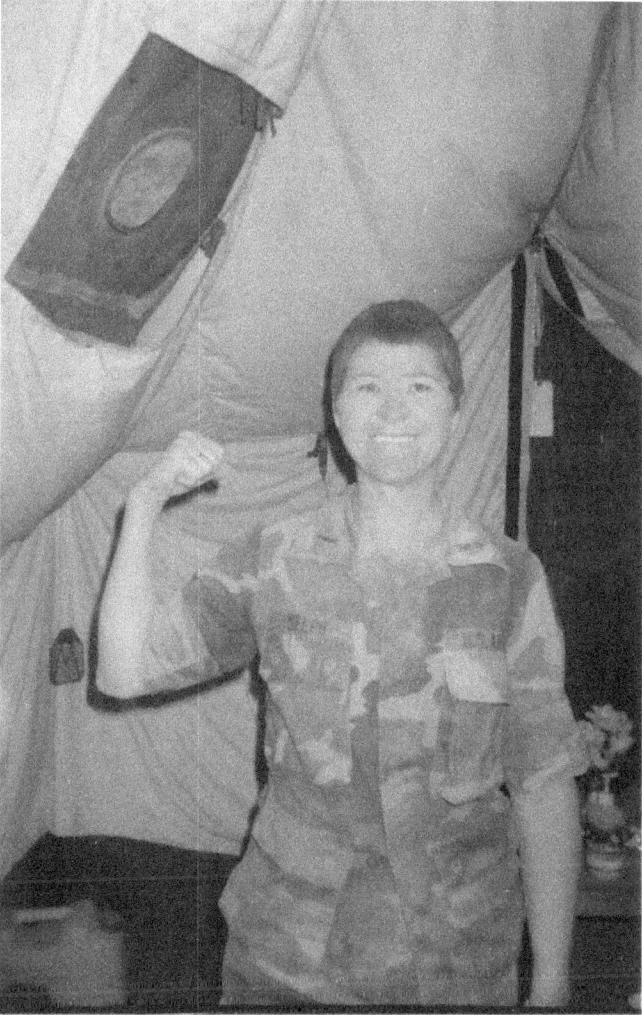
Figure 9: After a Dust Storm

Figure 10: On the Roof of Saddam's Palace

CERTS RECEIVED

Figure 11: Bronze Star Medal 2004

THE UNITED STATES OF AMERICA

TO ALL WHO SHALL SEE THESE PRESENTS, GREETING: THIS IS TO CERTIFY THAT THE PRESIDENT
OF THE UNITED STATES OF AMERICA AUTHORIZED BY EXECUTIVE ORDER, 24 AUGUST 1962 HAS AWARDED

THE BRONZE STAR MEDAL

LIEUTENANT COLONEL LEVONDA J. SELPH
UNITED STATES ARMY

TO

FOR EXCEPTIONALLY MERITORIOUS SERVICE AS THE COMMANDER AT TAJI NATIONAL SUPPLY DEPOT WITH THE MULTI-NATIONAL SECURITY TRANSITION COMMAND - IRAQ IN SUPPORT OF OPERATION IRAQI FREEDOM III FROM 14 APRIL 2005 TO 30 SEPTEMBER 2005. LIEUTENANT COLONEL SELPH'S TIRELESS EFFORTS COUPLED WITH HER TECHNICAL EXPERTISE MADE HER AN INVALUABLE MEMBER OF THE COMMAND. SHE DILIGENTLY AND EFFECTIVELY COORDINATED THE PLANNING AND DEVELOPMENT OF THE IRAQI ARMY NATIONAL SUPPLY DEPOT. HER DYNAMIC LEADERSHIP AND EXTRAORDINARY ACHIEVEMENTS WERE AN ESSENTIAL ELEMENT IN THE ESTABLISHMENT OF THE IRAQI SUPPLY INFRASTRUCTURE. HER DYNAMIC LEADERSHIP AND NUMEROUS ACHIEVEMENTS CONTRIBUTED SUBSTANTIALLY TO THE MULTI-NATIONAL SECURITY TRANSITION COMMAND-IRAQ MISSION OF DEVELOPING AND SUSTAINING IRAQI SECURITY FORCES. THE SINGULARLY OUTSTANDING ACCOMPLISHMENTS OF LIEUTENANT COLONEL SELPH HAVE BEEN IN KEEPING WITH THE HIGHEST TRADITIONS OF MILITARY SERVICE AND REFLECT DISTINCT CREDIT ON HER AND THE UNITED STATES ARMY.

GIVEN UNDER MY HAND IN THE CITY OF WASHINGTON
THIS 20TH DAY OF SEPTEMBER 2005

MARTIN E. DEMPSEY
LIEUTENANT GENERAL, US ARMY
COMMANDING GENERAL
MNSTC - IRAQ

Figure 12: Bronze Star Medal 2005

DEPARTMENT OF THE ARMY

THIS IS TO CERTIFY THAT THE SECRETARY OF THE ARMY HAS AWARDED

THE ARMY ACHIEVEMENT MEDAL

TO   LIEUTENANT COLONEL LEVONDA J. SELPH

FOR exceptionally meritorious service in the aftermath of 11 September 2001 attack. LTC Selph was in the Pentagon when the aircraft commandeered by terrorists hit the building. LTC Selph was among the Pentagon personnel who were evacuated from the building. LTC Selph was not immediately aware of the nature of the emergency. However, as soon as LTC Selph realized that it was a crisis situation, she volunteered for stretcher duty. LTC Selph, without any thought for her personal safety, continued to work the stretcher detail until no more victims remained. LTC Selph's courageous actions reflect great credit upon herself, the Office of the Deputy Chief of Staff, G-4; and the United States Army.

11 September 2001 to 11 September 2001
GIVEN UNDER MY HAND IN THE CITY OF WASHINGTON
This 25th Day of January 2002

Permanent Order #025-2
HQDA, ODCSLOG
The Pentagon
Washington, DC 20310-0500

CHARLES S. MAHAN, JR.
Lieutenant General, GS
Deputy Chief of Staff, G-4

Figure 13: The Army Achievement Medal 2001

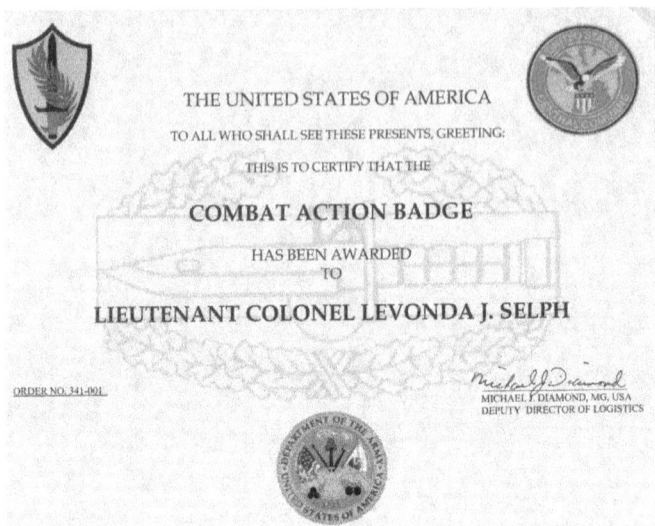

THE UNITED STATES OF AMERICA

TO ALL WHO SHALL SEE THESE PRESENTS, GREETING:

THIS IS TO CERTIFY THAT THE

COMBAT ACTION BADGE

HAS BEEN AWARDED
TO

LIEUTENANT COLONEL LEVONDA J. SELPH

ORDER NO. 341-001

MICHAEL J. DIAMOND, MG, USA
DEPUTY DIRECTOR OF LOGISTICS

Figure 14: Combat Action Badge—this is the award that separates those who went to combat, and those who fought in combat. To get this award, you had to have been in direct fire of the enemy. I got it for two direct fire fights I was in with the enemy after being hit with IEDs. For the grace of God, I survived.

CHAPTER 5

MY BATTLE WITH "MACHO" COLONEL

CHAPTER 5

MY BATTLE WITH "MACHO" COLONEL

Once again back in the United States, following the war, I found myself on active duty working as a Chief, Maintenance Branch, Command Logistics Review Team. This is an inspection team, and everybody on the team was in the ordnance maintenance career field. Maintenance Ordnance does the same for military vehicles, which is all maintenance requirements from A to Z in addition to keeping good records on all of the Army's equipment assigned to a unit. The inspection team that I lead was tasked to ensure that all the maintenance was properly performed, with records at each of the locations in which we visited throughout the United States, Virgin Islands, Guam, and Puerto Rico. An officer oversees or supervises the operations and completes reports for the higher echelon of command. The enlisted soldiers perform the actual maintenance functions, following regulations and maintaining the records. My team's job was to ensure the commands did just that. The purpose of the inspections was really to ensure the Army's equipment was kept in good running condition and, in addition, ready to mobilize in the event of war.

The job itself was going very well, and I loved it. We were scheduled to travel to every state in the union on a two year cycle, and I loved to travel; so the job was fitting for me in every way. The only unfortunate part of the job was that my boss and I did not get along very well. We were quite opposite in our views. I had gained a reputation of being fair and taking a "white hat" approach toward the inspections, and he had a reputation of preferring the "black hat" approach. It's kind of like a glass half full versus a glass half empty. Since he was the colonel and I just a captain, his half was really full. HA HA!

It was not unusual for organizations to compare notes on how well the inspection went and what the next organization should do prior to inspection in anticipation for the team's arrival. I tried to be positive, fair and help the organizations correct their discrepancies, and, as a result, the units liked my approach. They were always happy to see me arrive and took pretty good care of me while I was on an inspection visit. I was treated far better than the colonel, and he took extreme offense to this. He was a colonel with a big ego who felt that he should always receive the royal treatment; not me as a mere captain.

My dad had told me many quotes, and one of them was, "If you can't help someone or say something good about them, then don't say anything at all." That was one of the roots of how I was raised, and it bled over into my military life.

My theory was, and still is, that if you have a problem, you need to know what it is and then you can fix it. I also believed that the units should know why their way of doing things was wrong in accordance with Army regulations. This way, it would be best for everybody; they would know what was wrong, why it was wrong and then know how to fix it. In my opinion, this method would have a longer lasting effect on the soldier responsible for maintaining the equipment records.

However, the colonel didn't think that way. He took pride in giving the units we inspected a bad report. I gave them a chance to fix the problem rather than just giving them a bad report. Like many other officers who make it to full colonel, he addressed a problem by saying, "It is this way because I said so." He was quick to point out the problems but never explained to them or helped the soldiers find solutions.

The final straw that really divided us was when he wanted me to write a unit up for a deficiency that did not exist. I refused, and he had me removed from my position since I was only a captain at the time. It was unheard of to disobey a superior, but I knew the truth and would not belittle myself to bow to his wishes. Even though he was a colonel and I was a captain, he was also a quartermaster officer and I was an ordnance officer. I had also heard that he had a reputation of getting rid of females from his previous commands.

When we returned to our offices in Washington D.C., he called me into his office. He felt that I had showed him up, and with that, he gave me a counseling statement and told me I was no longer part of his team. Having been on the team for two years, I was shocked and very disappointed … it hurt my pride and self esteem a lot.

After thinking about it, I realized that I had done

nothing wrong and should not take this without a fight. I loved that job and did not want to leave. There's a process for discharging people from active duty, so while he was doing what he had to in order to follow the process, I filed an appeal to a special actions board, which stopped everything until the board results came back.

The results of the appeal were that I had been treated in an unfair and unjust manner, and anything negative that he had put in my records was to be removed.

Having won the battle, I requested a transfer to be in a different division away from him. At first, this request was denied, so I once again appealed and told the judge advocate and inspector general about the situation. In the end, the inspector general convinced the Division Chief to approve my transfer because he was told that if he didn't, I had a very good case for legal action.

Looking back, I could tell this particular colonel had some serious issues when it came to women. I recall a trip that our team took to Colorado, which at that time was a two week trip due to the size of the state and the number of units we had to inspect. It wasn't unusual to take long trips since the larger states took two weeks to complete a visit to all the units.

On the Friday, at the end of the first week, the colonel called a meeting and wanted to know who in the team wanted to climb Pike's Peak on Saturday. He got only two volunteers, a lieutenant colonel and me. I always liked a challenge, and since I had no other weekend plans, this seemed like a good one. I thought it would be a great way to stay in shape, get exercise and have fun doing it.

In case you don't know much about Pikes Peak, it's the

most visited mountain in North America and has a peak of 14,110 feet above sea level. It became famous during the gold rush of 1859 when gold rushers came up with the slogan, "Pikes Peak or bust."

So, we departed Colorado Springs early on Saturday morning with me driving the three us to the mountain. It wasn't hard to find after all its fame, and signs were everywhere. It was late in the fall, cold, and the peak was covered with snow. Foolish us, it became quite evident that we did not come to Pikes Peak with the proper equipment to climb a mountain of that size covered with snow.

As we climbed; the higher we got, the deeper the snow became; but, even without snowshoes, we did make it all the way to the top. By the time we got there, we were wading in snow waist deep.

On our way up, we ran into some (obviously professional) mountain climbers. The clue was that they had all of the right equipment: snow shoes, poles, snow suits, goggles and toboggans. When we met them, they were on their way back down, and we were going up (about three-fourths of the way to the top). The colonel was a total jerk to these people and was very insulting. He made statements to the effect that they were wimps, and it took a real man to climb the mountain without all that equipment. He made it known that he was a colonel in the Army and a "real man".

In actuality, he was being a "real jerk". While the lieutenant colonel stuck closely to the colonel, I was getting rather embarrassed to be seen with him, so I tried to separate myself from them by going on ahead. I got to the top first and heard him yelling at me to stay there until they reached the top, so I did.

As soon as they got to the top, I told him that I needed to keep moving because I felt like my toes were frozen and getting frostbite. The three of us proceeded to hike back down the snow-covered mountain.

About half-way down, the colonel said he needed to take a break and sat down on a log covered with snow. The lieutenant colonel sat down beside him. I told him that I had to keep moving to keep the blood flowing or I would freeze and get frost bite.

So, I took off by myself, hiking down the mountain toward the truck that we had parked at the bottom. God blessed me with a great sense of direction, and I had no trouble getting back.

I made it to a lake at the bottom of the peak and could see the truck parked on the other side of the lake. I followed a trail around the lake and arrived at a road within 50 yards of the truck. I still had the keys because I drove us up to Pikes Peak and thought I would be driving us back since I was the junior officer.

As I reached the road, I heard a voice behind me yelling my name. I stopped and turned around, it was the colonel. I stopped so he could catch up with me, but when he did, much to my surprise, he proceeded to chew my "you know what" off like I was a red-headed stepchild.

He said that I was in danger going off by myself, and for me to give him the keys, get in the back seat of the vehicle, and keep my mouth shut until the lieutenant colonel got to the truck. I did just that, and the lieutenant colonel showed up in about 20 minutes and drove us back to Colorado Springs.

They were laughing and joking in the front seat while I looked on, not allowed to open my mouth. I felt like I was being treated like a child and would have liked to start asking, "Are we there yet?" every ten minutes or so. Of course I didn't. I knew I was outranked, so I just sat quietly. The bottom line is that the colonel could not let a subordinate, much less a female, out do him.

When he fired me from the team, had me moved me to another division and gave me a less-than-desirable Officer Evaluation Report. Since he didn't have much of a case, he also based it on my inability to read, write and brief at the general officer level.

While preparing my appeal, thirty-five general officers, all of whom I had briefed, wrote letters on my behalf that basically stated that I was the best thing that had ever happened to the team and that my communications skills were exceptional. They also stated that I conducted myself in a professional manner and was always willing to help soldiers.

I had also enrolled in the General Staff Officer Course, which is a requirement during your captain or major years to progress, be competitive and get promoted to the next grade.

The English professor who had graded all my written assignments gave me A+'s on all my papers, once again proving that there was nothing wrong with my writing skills.

And you know the rest of the story; it was only a matter of time until women would ruffle the feathers of male officers. I was taught that prejudice was not acceptable and unbecoming behavior. My experience with prejudice against sex came at a time when my career meant the world to me and left deep wounds. The emotional pain would linger in my soul for the next several years. It was hard for me to trust anyone, because I felt ruthlessly and profoundly betrayed.

Deception happened one other time in my career. Trying to rationalize these distressing experiences was extremely difficult for me. I had been extremely loyal to the military to the point where I had been accused by some, of being married to my uniform. I finally decided the best thing for me to do was to move on and chalk these experiences up to the fact that certain men simply cannot deal with a strong and/or successful woman.

What I learned from the unpleasant experiences is that you really learn who your friends are when you face troubled waters. It seemed that all my peers were afraid to speak up or even be around me because the colonel might have see them supporting me, and the same thing could have happened to them. Each and every time that I have been on the upside of my career, people have wanted a part of the action; but as soon as I fell, I was avoided like the plague.

Next Stop, South Korea

When all of the nonsense with the colonel was behind me, I was assigned to the manpower division where officers conduct studies to determine how many soldiers are needed to accomplish a particular job. In my case, I did studies on manpower for maintenance facilities. When determining how many mechanics are needed in a maintenance facility, you must know the amount of equipment to be maintained in addition to the time it takes to maintain each piece of equipment. After two years in this position, I was promoted to major but still wanted to get ahead. That said, I took an assignment that nobody else wanted ... in South Korea. This assignment was what is called "non-accompanied", which means family members cannot go along. The position focused on writing wartime host nation support plans, which are plans that explained what South Korea would provide for the United States if they went to war with North Korea.

I was in Korea for two years, and there were numerous meetings with the South Koreans. I must say, whenever there are different languages spoken and interpreters involved, everything takes twice as long to complete. Going back and forth through interpreters doubles the time involved.

My job was coordinating and planning the logistics support requirements for everything in the event of conflict. Since things changed periodically, I needed to keep updating my plans accordingly. One year, they'd support you in one way, and the next year they may decide to do something else.

It was kind of slow moving, but since I was assigned there for awhile, I wasn't in any great hurry. I was content with the job and seeing another part of the world. I did manage to publish the first wartime host nation support plans that had been staffed and approved by both governments in over ten years.

When I first arrived in Korea, I needed to find housing. Depending on your grade, you would have a certain per diem allowance for an apartment. For me, it was $1,600 per month. Of course the local nationals who rented apartments to U.S. military personnel were aware of this, so they would charge the maximum amount. I looked at about thirty apartments before I found one that I thought I could deal with. Most that I saw were extremely small or dirty, or both. The one I ended up with was about 600 square feet with two small bedrooms and no closets. Since I worked a lot, I figured this could be a plus because I would have less to clean. None of the apartments had closets; instead, they had a wardrobe chest where you could hang up your clothes. I made one of the bedrooms into an office, and this was home for my entire two year stay.

The people I rented from were very nice and treated me very well. They owned a pharmacy below two apartments, and they lived in the one that I was not renting. The gentleman also did acupuncture in the back of the pharmacy. As it turned out, they also had three children living in Los Angeles who were each pharmacists. At least I knew that if I got sick, I could probably get medication.

In fact, I had some kind of skin bacteria at one point, so my landlord did acupuncture on me in an effort to help. It was some sort of bacteria that would stay with me for over fifteen years; and unfortunately, the acupuncture did not work, but it was quite an interesting experience. Later speculation from a dermatologist hypothesized that the bacteria was caused from taking showers in Desert Storm from the water hauled by fuel tankers that had not been properly purged.

While I was in Southwest Asia, because of the job, I did get to travel around and see South Korea. There were some poor rural areas and some major modern cities.

Seoul, home to nearly 10 million people, is the nation's largest city and the capital. It's very congested with cars, mopeds and bicycles everywhere.

I got a moped after I had been in Seoul for two months to help get around, but you had to be very careful when riding since there were some crazy drivers over there. Prices weren't cheap either. In fact, Seoul is now considered the sixth-most expensive city in the world to live, and I'm sure at that time—in the late 1990s—it wasn't much different.

I also got to take a bus tour to the demilitarized zone (DMZ) that separates the North Korea from South Korea. It's interesting to see a guard on each side of the breach, only about 200 feet apart. The two guards would talk to each other by phone, waving to one another, and seemed quite friendly. Who knows, maybe they were friends or even relatives separated by politics but had no real problems with each other.

What I also found interesting was that every year, for the past 40 years, the North Koreans cross over and fish in South Korean waters, and they don't seem to really mind that much. Our own government seems to have more interest in where North Korea fishes than the South Koreans. Apparently, at certain times of the year, the fishing is more plentiful in these waters.

I thought about how our state department chose to report something like this recently, stating that the North Koreans were seen in South Korean waters. In my opinion, it's like they are trying to stir up propaganda. What they don't say is that this has been going on for forty years and will probably keep going on for the next forty years unless the fish schools shift to other waters.

What probably happens is that someone in the state department thinks this is unusual and makes a story out if it because he's not over there in person to see what is really going on. Looking at the newspaper stories and knowing what it's really like in South Korea now makes me think of the crap I'm going through, and the difference between knowing the truth and hearing what the media and the politicians have to say. It's the same case with Iraq; they don't know what goes on over there. They make up stories to fit their political agendas, and I got caught up in one such mess.

Anyway, when I was getting ready to leave Korea, the couple renting me the apartment—the pharmacist couple—took me out for dinner. We went to a very nice restaurant. I don't know exactly what they ordered; then again, I didn't know what I was eating half the time while I was over there. I just ate it to be polite and did not ask questions for fear that they would have been offended. What I can say is that everything they ordered was very tasty and authentic.

What was most amusing was when we returned home, they took me to a pub that was in the basement of the pharmacy. Having lived there for two years, I never knew it was there. I didn't go out at night because it was very noisy and rowdy outside. You could tell there was a lot of drinking going on, and it was not unusual to hear fights in the streets or some guy beating up his wife. I just felt safer inside my apartment with my doors locked.

But when my landlords took me to karaoke, I felt safe with them. The gentlemen sang, and even though I didn't know what song he was singing, it sounded pretty good. It was a nice send off, and they were genuinely sad to see me leave.

Apparently, I must have done a good job in South Korea because shortly after I returned to the United States, the senior advisor recommended me for a promotion. I was promoted to lieutenant colonel in June 2000 while attending the Logistics Executive Development Course at Fort Lee, Virginia. Only the best logisticians get to go to this course, and I felt very much honored.

Returning to Stateside

After Korea, I was also awarded an Army commendation medal, and my career was continuing to move forward. I was also assigned to a position in the Pentagon, which I would start after the six months of school at Fort Lee was completed. Unlike other military schools, this was not a physical endeavor, but instead the focus was on everything you could ever want to know about logistics from A to Z, including leadership, forms, regulations, and so on. I was up to my neck in logistics, but I liked it and found it challenging with a great learning opportunity.

Then, in December of 2000, I started working at the Pentagon. There was something very exciting about working there, and it took a while to get the necessary clearance.

Each morning, I would get up early and head from my townhouse in Alexandria, Virginia, down Interstate 395 in attempt to beat the early morning traffic congestion. I managed to arrive each day just as my chosen building entrance opened, many times passing by the usual protestors who made a habit of gathering outside of the Pentagon, even when we were not at war. I guess they were just protesting the military in general. They would camp out on the Pentagon steps—at that time, security was still not too tight in the parking lots. All of that would soon change.

The learning curve was steep, and I eventually had eight programs to sponsor and oversee. Each one of these programs had history, and to support them, I had to learn that history. I went to many briefings that helped me to learn and understand each one. I also went to many briefings presented by contractors that were new but needed funding.

The contracting and funding came from other divisions since I was not in contracting or finance but rather a logistician. All I could do was make recommendations at the Program Objective Memorandum (POM) Boards (a group of finance and contracting officers). Although, I found more redundancies in new programs than not and don't remember ever recommending a new program for funding.

I worked in the logistics information systems branch, utilizing some of what I had just learned in the Logistics Executive Development Course. One of my first tasks was to complete a study and determine what a subordinate agency—Logistics Integration Agency (LIA)—was doing in terms of innovation and expenditures, i.e. budgeting and monitoring the spending of money. It was not unusual for the Chief of (then) LIA to make testimonies on the hill for funding to support various projects.

As it turned out, the Chief of LIA and the Deputy Chief

of Staff for Logistics had a rivalry of sorts going back well before I was assigned to the division. While it's probably true of any major company or business, it's particularly true in the military to find a lot of big egos.

The Chief of LIA would do things the general did not know about, which included spending money, and the general should have been briefed but was not. In reality, it wasn't like they were throwing money away; they were just doing what they wanted to without the general's approval.

LIA's mission was to research areas for new development that would help the logistics community and would make it work better from a technological aspect. They had numerous programs that I was monitoring at one time plus a lot of hidden programs, so I had to do my research to prepare a briefing.

I later became a program sponsor on the Army staff, so I would go before a board and brief my projects for budget purposes every other year. It was a two year cycle—one year, you receive the funding to support your program, followed by a briefing for new funding requirements the next year. The cycle process is a call Program, Objective, Memorandum (POM). The purpose of the POM is to ensure the Department of Defense's priorities are met with available funding, which is never enough to do everything that needs to be done.

I figured the best way to brief my program requirement was to go strictly as I was taught in earlier training and by the book in regard to format. Since people seldom go by the book when briefing at higher levels, the chairman of the board thought it was refreshing and was very impressed with my briefing. He told his counterparts that my briefing was the way it is supposed to be done.

Things at the Pentagon were going well. I received my first general officer top block Officer Evaluation Report. Senior raters are only allowed to give five percent (5%) of their subordinates' top blocks, which means you are the best among your pay grade at your job. I did not expect a "top block" and was totally surprised when I received my review. The general officer who gave it to me assured me that I had earned the exceptional evaluation.

During my Pentagon tour, I had very little social life to speak of, working from the time the doors opened until 7 or 8 o'clock at night; but as a lieutenant colonel, I felt proud that I had achieved my goal of working my way up the ladder. Of course, there were always more steps to climb, and I was looking forward to what was in store. Little did I or anyone else know, at that time, that within a year of my employment at the Pentagon, the world would soon be changed forever, and I would be right in the middle of it … literally!

CHAPTER 6

9/11/2001
TRAGEDY IN THE PENTAGON
AND AT MY HOME FRONT

CHAPTER 6

9/11/2001
TRAGEDY IN THE PENTAGON
AND AT MY HOME FRONT

The date was December 01, 2000 when I first walked into Room 4C348 in the Pentagon. Due to renovations, by the grace of God, I was moved to 3C367 on August 11, 2001. This is the third corridor of the third floor in ring C.

The first nine months of my Pentagon tour were spent working for the Deputy Chief of Staff for Logistics in corridor four. Our move to corridor three took two full days of packing and moving, and that was with the help of professional contract movers. Unbeknownst to any of us on that summer day, this move would turn out to be the saving grace for my coworkers and myself.

One month—to the day—after moving offices, the Pentagon was attacked as American Airlines Flight 77, which would completely destroy the area where my old office had been prior to August 11, 2001. The move saved my life as well as the lives of my logistics coworkers.

It was 8:45 a.m., the morning of September 11, 2001,

and I was in room 3C367, my new office space in the Pentagon. The division chief had scheduled our normal morning staff meeting for 9:00 a.m. in the Logistics Automation Division conference room.

I went into Colonel T.R.'s office and told him that I was going to the Red Skin's Snack Bar on the fifth corridor—a run for a cup of coffee and would be back in time for the staff meeting.

I briskly walked the halls to the fifth corridor and got the coffee, but as I went through the checkout, the cashier, an Aramark employee, said she had heard that a plane had flown into the twin towers (The World Trade Center) in New York City. I brushed her off and told her that it had to be a rumor, because if it were true, I would have heard about it.

Moments later, I returned to the colonel's office where everyone had gathered to watch the news. The capture was a review of the plane flying into the twin towers, just as the cashier had said. Everyone was in disbelief.

I commented when I realized what had happened, "If they could do that to the twin towers, the Pentagon is also a target."

The staff broke away from the television and went into the conference room for the scheduled meeting. What was different this time from other meetings was that the deputy chaired the meeting, and the colonel was in a meeting with the 3-star general over all logistics divisions.

We sat down, and the deputy had just finished going over the agenda when an incredible boom shook the building like an earthquake.

The room instantly filled with deep, thick, black smoke.

I could not see two feet in front of me. My coworkers were screaming, crying and running out of the room. I was somewhat in shock not knowing what it was that hit us, and trying not to panic. I sat in my seat in shock for what seemed like minutes, but was probably not more than 20 seconds. By the time I decided to get up and find out what was happening, no one else was in the conference room, or in the office for that matter.

I felt my way through the dark smoke to the hall, where I found it was filled with people packed like sardines. In the darkened halls, I could hear screams and people crying as they tried to get out. Having worked there for nearly a year, and having a good sense of direction, I knew where the exits were even in the blackout caused by the smoke and the loss of lights. With the hordes of people, we all headed in the direction of the courtyard in the center of the Pentagon to escape the smoke in hopes of safety.

When I got to the courtyard, people were packed shoulder to shoulder. I saw a couple of guys with their heads bleeding with some fragments of heavy-gauge metal, but still did not know what had happened.

I found two coworkers who said they thought a bomb had gone off in the fifth corridor, then someone told us that a plane had flown into the building. I later saw larger metal fragments about a foot long and two feet wide.

I told my coworkers that we needed to get out of the courtyard because if one plane already hit us, the next one could kill us all in the courtyard. I felt like a pig in a pen waiting to be slaughtered.

We tried to get back inside the building through a couple of different corridor doors, but security had locked all the doors from inside. We worked our way around to the ninth corridor, where we finally made our way back into the building. Everyone was moving toward the metro exit, and we followed the crowd.

When we got to the metro exit, we were shuttled outside to the east end parking lot. From there, we were directed to go across the interstate to Pentagon City, which is basically a shopping mall with restaurants and so on, located across interstate 395.

When I got to Pentagon City, I tried to find a telephone to call relatives to let them know I was alright, but all of the phones had lines at least 20 deep waiting to make calls to their loved ones. I had left my cell phone in my car that morning, and the south parking lot where it had been placed was locked down for security reasons. My two-week-old Lexus RX 300 was locked in, and I was now walking. We were never allowed to bring cell phones into the Pentagon for security reasons and the concern that someone may record or photograph classified information.

At this point, I was still not completely sure what had happened, but I worked my way outside the Pentagon shopping area and headed toward Army-Navy Drive in Pentagon City. As I got to Army-Navy Drive, you could see the flames and billowing black smoke pouring out of the Pentagon.

Suddenly, a police car stopped on the Interstate 395 overpass. A police officer got out of the car and pulled out a bull horn. He told the thousands of people below to clear the area and that another plane was spotted heading our way. Speculation had it that the plane was targeting the White House or the Capitol Building in the District of Washington. Again, people began running in every direction away from Pentagon City.

I later learned that this was the plane that went down in Pennsylvania. It was later reported and confirmed to have been headed for the White House.

I started briskly walking with two of my coworkers toward the Army-Navy Country Club, about a half-mile away, where I had an affiliate membership. There was suddenly another huge bang that shook the ground in Pentagon City, and I thought it was a bomb going off in Washington D.C.

We made it to the country club—now nearly 1:00 p.m.—and everyone was watching the news in one of the restaurants. It was then and there that I found out what had really happened. I also learned that the loud boom I had heard earlier was a fighter jet breaking the sound barrier as it took off from Andrews Air Force Base, and it was not another attack.

I was able to use a phone from the office of the country club to call family members and let them know I was alright. The management at the country club also allowed my friends to call their families.

The lieutenant colonel who was with me came out of the country club office crying when he got off the phone with his family. After contacting our families, we had sandwiches, which I paid for with a chit, then continued to watch the news in disbelief.

An announcement came on the air that requested military personnel to return to the Pentagon to assist with the rescue efforts of the victims of the attack who were still in the building. I quickly finished my sandwich, received a ride down Army-Navy Drive on a golf cart, and walked the rest of the way back to the Pentagon.

I walked past my Lexus RX 300, which was still in lock down in the Pentagon south parking lot. The car was parked two spaces from the flight path of the plane that had crashed into the building. It was covered with black soot from the fire, which was still burning, but it was otherwise not-damaged.

I saw many ambulances and fire trucks, and there were numerous people—police officers, rescue workers and military personnel—all performing rescue duties while firefighters continued to fight the blaze. I was in uniform and had my ID with me, so I was allowed into the area without question.

I went over and fell in on stretcher detail. First, a body covered with a sheet needed to be moved from the building to an ambulance. From that first stretcher to many others, people continued to be taken out of the blazing building and driven to hospitals all over D.C. and the surrounding areas. The casualties had sheets pulled over their heads, and the many injured were lying on stretchers bleeding, crying and praying.

I was still in shock as this became a robotic task that continued for nearly eight more hours, until around 8 p.m. At that point, I walked to Pentagon City where the metro was still running, and I got on a train en route to my home in Alexandria, Virginia.

When I got on the metro, I saw a colonel who worked with me in the Pentagon that looked like a ghost and was obviously still in shock. I later learned that he had been inside the Pentagon building, pulling out the bodies that I and others had been carrying on stretchers to the ambulances for recovery outside the building.

When I got to Alexandria, I stopped to get something to eat at a well-known restaurant on Kings Street along the metro line in Alexandria, Virginia. I had not had anything to eat since I had left the Army-Navy Country Club earlier that morning. The restaurant was called Theismann's—named after Joe Theismann, the famous football star.

While at the restaurant, I met an intern who worked for one of the US Senators. She gave me her card, but I was so numb that I ended up losing it and do not remember her name.

After ordering, I realized that I had no appetite, so I got back on the metro. It was 10:30 before I got home that evening, still somewhat in shock and disbelief myself.

When I finally got home, I turned on the television, and that's when it really hit me—the United States of America had been attacked. I felt like a total failure and wanted nothing more than revenge for the "bastards" who did this to my "Mother Land". When you wear a uniform in defense of this country, you take this very seriously. I had spent my life defending this country, and the terrorists had defeated my twenty years of effort in just a few short hours.

I cried for three hours non-stop until I finally fell asleep in a chair in the living room, watching the news. I only slept for a few hours that night and the next four or five nights.

The day after 9/11, I returned some fifteen phone calls

from friends and relatives that were on my answering machine, asking if I was okay. Even though I wasn't really okay, I let them know that I had indeed survived and was safe, or at least as safe as anyone could feel after the attack. To be honest, I still felt, and even feel to this day, that it's not a matter of "if" something like this is going to happen again, but when. I couldn't understand how there was no clearance for these people getting pilots training and licenses or how this horrific event could happen with the technology and the level of sophistication and with the intelligence that we have today. How could we, the United States, let ourselves become so vulnerable and victimized by terrorists?

The events of 9/11 were extremely hard on my mother. I was unable to call her to let her know I was alright until after midnight on September 12. I knew she did not have a clue about some of the conditions I had worked in, nor that any of them could have been life threatening. I never wanted her to worry, so I did not tell her much about my various assignments over the past years. After 9/11, she became very ill and passed away the next year. My boss in the Pentagon learned of Mom's illness and allowed me to be with her during her six-month hospital stay. Her death was extremely hard on me because Mom had become my best friend. After her death, I felt an emptiness that I continue to carry seven years later.

I made a promise to myself after 9/11 that I would do everything within my power to fight terrorism even if it meant giving my own life.

Business as Usual?

We were back to work in an off-site building two days after 9/11. I was allowed to recover my vehicle, and plans were underway to get our lives back to normal, or at least as normal as could be under these conditions.

The site where we were to work was located in the Army Material Command, a subordinate command to U.S. Army, which was located in a building on Eisenhower Avenue in Alexandria, Virginia. The entire division shared one room with plywood dividers as our new office space.

For the first few days, without phones, computers or our files, we really couldn't do any work, but we did talk about what had happened, and we were all still in shock. The incredible, forceful fires continued to burn for several days at the Pentagon. Our boss wanted us to proceed with everything as close to normal as possible, but it was very hard.

Shortly after 9/11, a long list of the casualties from the attack was posted in the Pentagon Mall hallway, which served as a grim reminder of what we had been through. I knew one person on the list.

Finally, they installed phones and computer hookups in our new office spaces on Eisenhower Avenue. Dell Computers donated workstations to the military for use, as a result of the tragedy.

After a few days, we were allowed back into the Pentagon to collect our personal belongings and our files. We all wore plastic suits to try to prevent any health hazards due to the mold and mildew from the water soaked and smoked rooms. It was strange going back into the building; everything was covered with soot, and the water damage from the firemen spraying everything to put out the blaze left you in more disbelief. We had to move around the burned, damaged structure. It was nothing like I had ever experienced before, or had even dreamt of for that matter.

My car was still dirty from the smoke, but it ran just fine, and I had it detailed shortly thereafter. I still have this car today and refuse to part from it because it is a constant reminder of that grim day in 2001.

It was a month before we finally moved back into our offices inside the Pentagon, and even at that point, corridors 2 through 7 were roped off. The damage of the impact area was primarily in corridors 4, 5 and 6, and all of these areas needed to be completely renovated.

It took some time to adjust to working in the Pentagon again. Everyone was fearful that something like this—something we had never thought possible—could happen again. Even on September 11, 2002—the one year anniversary—I worked off-site at Fort Belvoir, Virginia just to be away from the Pentagon and feel safe.

Assignment Waiting Game

I remember waiting for the president's response to 9/11, knowing that we had to do something. I believe President Bush did a lot of soul searching before making any decision that would affect the future of the United States. When he finally made his decision to go to war in Afghanistan, I felt that he made the right decision to go after the terrorists. I did not believe he had much of a choice, given they had attacked our Mother soil. We did not attack them and it was only right that we defend our nation. I also felt compelled to go to Afghanistan, or later to Iraq, but my assignment at the Pentagon did not end until June of 2003.

Most of my work after the attack on 9/11 was in a highly secured area of the Pentagon. I worked the night shift and stayed every morning for a briefing in which I helped prepare for the Deputy Chief of Staff for Logistics. A lot had happened with the war in both Afghanistan and Iraq. The three-star General was responsible for supplying the Army components engaged in the wars with all, Classes of Supply, which is a logistics function.

I remember one of the most upsetting things that the three-star General had to contend with was soldiers appearing on the news channels wearing mixed uniforms. I also remember General Shinseki telling the Secretary of Defense that the Army needed 500,000 troops to success-fully accomplish the mission at hand in Iraq. It would later prove to be an accurate assessment on General Shinseki's part. I later got the opportunity to witness firsthand the shortage of manpower to complete the tasks given in the combat driven sands of Iraq.

When it was time for my next assignment, in the spring of 2003, I waited to see where I was going to be moved to next. The officer making the decisions over my next assignment was very contradictory. If you said white, he would say black, if you said black, he would say white. He always had to have the last word, and that was just part of his nature. I believe he thought his decisions were for the good of the Army, but like many military leaders that have an ego and can't give in to not being in charge. That type of leadership sometimes gets in the way of making the best decisions for the organization.

By February 2003, I was getting anxious. I still didn't have my orders, and the war had already started. I figured if I wanted to get assigned overseas, I'd have to use some reverse psychology on the boss. So I mentioned to him that I had read that there was a 75% shortage of logistics officers in Afghanistan, and that I was afraid and really didn't want that assignment. He responded, "I really don't give a damn what you want ... you're going."

He got the last word, and I got what I wanted. I continued to work in the Pentagon until May of 2003.

CHAPTER 7

IRAQ – HERE I COME!

CHAPTER 7

IRAQ – HERE I COME!

I thought I was heading for Afghanistan since the intelligence reports I had reviewed stated there was a shortage of logistics officers in that theater of operations, Although, my new assignment came with orders sending me to Central Command Headquarters, MacDill Air Force Base in Tampa, Florida. I quickly and anxiously went house hunting in Tampa and found a new home without any problems. It was much easier than house hunting had been in Korea since everything was cleaner, and there were even closets in all the homes, not to mention everyone spoke English in Tampa.

My new job was a Logistics Plans Officer under the Deputy Chief of Staff for Logistics. My job would be to write logistics plans for Iraq while based in Tampa. But before I could even settle in, within one week of my new assignment, General Abizaid let it be known that he wanted a team of experts in various fields to go to Baghdad and be his eyes and ears forward.

General Abizaid was one of the most respected generals in the military. He was the four-star Unified Commander of US Central Command (CENTCOM).

His responsibility was to oversee operations in more than two dozen countries around the world with three of them in conflict during his command. At this point, in 2003, he had already been in the military for thirty-one years.

As it turned out, nobody in the logistics community volunteered … except for me, so I was chosen to go to Iraq. I would be on the Operations Plans and Coordination Cell (OPCC) for General Abizaid.

While most of the soldiers were sent to a mobilization station where they were prepared for the combat conditions and given additional instructions that might be required to perform in Iraq or Afghanistan, I did not receive any special training prior to deployment. I did, however, have to go through a deployment physical to ensure that I was physically fit, but that was about it. I passed my physical and was ready to leave for Baghdad in June 2003.

My family thought I was crazy for volunteering, but nothing could convince me that I was not doing the right thing. My friends thought I was a hero with lots of courage to volunteer when I certainly did not have to do so. I felt obligated to go with the intention of deterring terrorism after the 9/11 attack. Furthermore, many soldiers who had less experience had to go whether they liked it or not. They simply did not have a choice. I saw many cowards in Central Command who sat back like fat ducks without giving a second thought to letting those kids go to combat and fight, while they stayed in their safe haven. I was never that way, but rather wanted to do whatever I could to ensure the safety of a fellow soldier in combat. In fact, when I did go to Iraq, I performed the life-threatening tasks that I would not let the soldiers under me do because of the high risk to life. I felt obligated to protect those under my supervision. I would not ask a soldier to do anything that I would not first do myself. That is what a good leader does, or at least that is what I was conditioned to believe and still do.

Baghdad, Iraq

When we first landed in Baghdad, it was just myself and four or five other soldiers who worked in other than logistics disciplines. The executive officer for OPCC, a marine lieutenant colonel, who first met us at Baghdad International Airport saw me and asked what I was doing in Iraq. He was obviously someone who did not believe that females should be in a combat theater of operations. Women in the combat zones was something that was still new for the military and hard for many male soldiers, especially those who had been in the military for many years—old school—to accept. I explained that I was the logistics representative for OPCC. Regardless of my position, he gave me a tough time in the beginning.

The bird colonel over our cell briefed General Abizaid, and the commander would come in roughly once every other month or so and meet and greet us and talk about the operations.

I recall one visit where he came in, and our chief wanted a picture of the OPCC staff with General Abizaid. Since I was the only female, I was trying to stay out of sight, basically keeping a low profile. I stood in the back of the room. I was never a straphanger or trying to brown-nose to get tight with the general. Surprisingly, when they got ready to take the picture, the general came over and stood right beside me. I felt about six inches tall, but was really taller than General Abizaid with my five-feet, six-inch frame.

Camp Victory is located at the Baghdad International Airport Camp, now called Camp International. It was probably the largest camp and became the best known because the USO shows would stop there. I actually met Drew Carey and his cast at Camp Victory, and believe it or not, I had never heard of him before. When everyone was ranting and raving over meeting Drew Carey, I was wondering *Who Is Drew Carey?* I was never a TV buff as it seemed like a waste of time for me. I was always working to promote my education and/or career.

The other OPCC staff was in Saddam's former palace in the International Green Zone about twelve miles from Camp Victory, where I would visit for staff call once a week. They had pretty neat quarters, trailers with bathrooms, beds, showers, etc.—much better than where I was in Camp Victory living in a tent. Nonetheless, I got by and did not complain, since my job was more important than any personal needs, or so I thought.

Most camps covered at least 100 acres. Many of the base camps had tents for sleeping quarters in early 2003-2004, but not in the IZ. As time went on, small trailers with a bathroom were found in some of the camps, but since there were not enough for everyone, the most senior officers got the trailers first. Once all the trailers were occupied, you would fend for yourself, which meant sleeping in a tent, in your vehicle or finding someone who had an extra room. Most of the soldiers were taken care of because they were deployed with a unit. It was different for me because I was on temporary duty orders from Central Command Headquarters and not on a deployment order or assigned to a deployed unit.

I was still considered a Central Command asset while deployed on temporary duty to Iraq, and many times I was questioned, "What the H___ are you doing here?"

There were security guards at the camps' entrances and exits. The guards were armed with various weapons and searched every vehicle for explosives prior to allowing them to come inside the perimeter. They also had dogs that sniffed every vehicle for drugs, weapons or explosives.

Everyone had to show a valid ID prior to going inside the secured perimeter. Mortars were fired into the camp daily, and during 2003–2004, this started at around 8:00–9:00 p.m. and again around 4:00 a.m. Sometimes, the terrorists would get lucky and hit a trailer or wipe out 20 or so vehicles in the parking lot.

Vehicles were only allowed to be parked in designated parking areas. In late 2004, or early 2005, a mortar went through part of the palace roof and killed one of my friends who was a female civilian. Even in the safest parts of Iraq, there was still a need to be prepared for daily and nightly indirect mortar fire.

Inside the camp perimeters became known as the Green Zone or safe zones because they were secured with armed guards and Bradley tanks. Outside the Green Zone is called the red zone since that is where the terrorists reside and will kill you at the drop of a hat if they know you are an American or part of the coalition.

In 2003, there were 37 coalition nations participating in the fight against terrorism in Iraq. The largest show of force was from the United States, followed by the British forces.

In time, the Green Zone became more secure but still remained a potential threat from constant and unpredictable mortar attack.

In 2004, some vendors and fast food courts established operations in the Green Zone of Iraq. While I was there on my third tour of temporary duty, we had Subway, Popeye's Chicken and Burger King. Our meals had been (and still were) furnished by contract dining facilities, but that got old after a while because it was the same old thing day after day, and a good old Burger King Whopper sure tasted good every now and then just for a change.

Working in a war zone, I would go to the briefings, return to Camp Victory and do what I needed for the upcoming week. We would identify logistics problems that the general could possibly do something about and more or less keep him informed on what was going well and what was not so well. Essentially, as previously stated, we were his eyes and ears on the ground, letting him know what was going on from the ground combat zone standpoint.

After about two months, I wrote one paper about the Iraqi military, the police, facility protective services and the Iraqi border patrol. All of these were needed in the Iraq infrastructure, but they didn't seem to exist since Saddam was in control of everything prior to the invasion in 2003. You comply with Saddam's rules, or you die. We were trying to get the Iraqis to take more responsibility for protecting their own country from the terrorists, but they didn't have a clue about what to do or how to follow our lead. If you've never seen a cop before, how can you be a cop?

Other than Saddam's republican army, nobody else in Iraq had uniforms. The Iraqi police were basically just people who did whatever Saddam Hussein had told them to do, following his laws. There was no real form of government, no uniforms, no training, nothing outside of Saddam's own forces. So, I included all of this in my paper in hopes of getting the Iraqi police and military trained and equipped with some structure to basically provide security for their country.

Apparently, the general liked what I wrote because I was moved after two weeks to the Baghdad palace where the logistics plans for the Iraqis were taking place ... to a great extent. The coalition logistics plans and operations remained at Camp Victory inside the perimeter of Baghdad International Airport.

The palace in Baghdad was a huge and incredible structure. It was like a real version of Caesars Palace in Las Vegas, except instead of hotel guests looking to win money, the palace was now loaded with coalition forces trying to turn Iraq into a more civilized nation without the influx of terrorists.

There were more than 100 rooms in the palace, some very ornate with painted ceilings and lavish designs. Although, we discovered that the crystal-looking chandeliers hanging from the high ceilings were really made of plastic. There was a full basement and two full stories inside the fortress. My guess is that it covered five acres easily. Yet, it was still not large enough for all the planning and operations offices required for support of the military, civilian and government contract personnel. So, the military put up plywood partitions to divide the rooms into office spaces. Many contractors were hired to establish communications for internet and telephone networks. One of the large rooms was used for a dining facility and had a seating capacity of roughly 300 personnel. Later, in 2005, the State Department took over the palace and most of the military moved to other locations within the International Green Zone.

The International Green Zone was and remains highly secured. I had one small warehouse inside the Green Zone in late 2003, and a mortar came in one night, hit it and blew a big hole in the roof. The supplies and materials had to be moved immediately to avoid theft and pilferage.

In early 2004, I wrote the plans for other warehouses to be colocated with Iraqi police training camps in Tikrit, Mosul, Ar Ramadi, Basrah, and the Baghdad Police Academy. In 2005, other warehouses were added to the logistics infrastructure at Taji and Babylon. All of these warehouses were where equipment, weapons and uniforms were sent to for what would become the Iraqi police, border patrol and facility protective services (better known as rent-a-cops). These camps are where Iraqis were trained to handle such jobs as managing traffic and enforcing the laws of the new Iraqi government. Of course, this meant that I had to go out to the warehouses often to ensure the management and issuing of equipment and weapons was done accurately with proper accountability and precise documentation. The last thing we wanted was the weapons landing in the hands of the terrorist.

For me, this also meant traveling on the roads from one base to another through towns and small cities in unsecured (red) zones, where terrorists could be lurking anywhere. I was in a red zone almost every day that I was in Iraq.

Performing logistics movement required a lot of traveling throughout the country. After I moved to Taji in early 2005, I had over ten Iraqi contractors come to meet me, and I had to go outside the Green Zone, find them and escort them inside the secured perimeter. Otherwise, the contractors would attempt to get inside the gates of the perimeter and, many times, fail.

The lines were long every morning, and getting inside the camp was on a first come, first serve basis for vehicle search and sniffing dogs. If someone like myself did not take decisive action to get the contractors inside the gate to perform the work for which they were hired, they might have never gotten cleared for entrance. This was extremely dangerous because the terrorists routinely attacked and killed anyone outside the gates of a Green Zone—especially anyone they knew or believed was helping the United States.

The consequence of not getting the contractors cleared was that they would charge the government as if they had performed, i.e., they showed up for work, and it was no fault of their own that our security forces did not allow them entrance to perform.

The daily challenge of getting anything done was a nightmare, but I refused to fail any mission. In my mind, missing a mission could cost us the life of a soldier, and that was too big of a price for me to be responsible for, even if it meant my own life was in jeopardy.

I had an American friend from Oklahoma and a British friend who were killed in the red zone on their way back from Tikrit in April of 2005. The terrorist drove up behind them and sprayed their vehicle with an AK-47, killing both instantly. But even way before that, I knew the dangers of traveling in these areas of Iraq. However, for me to do my job, extreme risk to my safety was unavoidable.

While working in the palace in 2003–04, I started working more closely with the Minister of the Interior. He was the head honcho over the Iraqi police, border patrol and facility protective services.

My job was to get logistics support to the training sites, and issue weapons and equipment to the graduating candidates. I didn't really have any help until May of 2004, but program managers and trainers were ordering a lot of materials for the Iraqi police, unknown to me. But now that billions of dollars worth of weapons and equipment were coming into theater, it became my responsibility to move, secure, account for, and issue to the Iraqi graduates.

One senior executive civilian service employee from the State Department did help me in 2003 and did a super job. That said, the two of us needed at least two hundred personnel, and growing, to do what the two of us were charged with in support to the Minister of the Interior. The SES and I did all the wholesale distribution of weapons and radios for the Iraqi police to support the first currency exchange. The two of us loaded trucks for three days, near non-stop. The Saddam currency was out as well as the new Iraq dinar—now the official currency as of January 2004.

Of course, each time I would get things going in the right direction to support the logistics infrastructure for the Ministry of the Interior, I got pulled back to Central Command in Tampa, Florida. Since I was on temporary duty, I could not work more than 179 days on a temporary duty order, otherwise, it would've been considered a Permanent Change of Station in accordance with military regulations.

Home for the Holidays

The first time I was pulled back to Tampa was in November 2003. I was home for the holidays with a mission largely unfinished overseas. I wanted to help with the war effort and did not feel that I was doing my duty as a soldier stationed in Tampa, Florida. The holidays that year were not very meaningful; I knew that I would be returning to Iraq and was preparing for my second deployment.

When I was involved in the war effort, every day was pretty much the same with little thought of anything except getting the mission, as assigned, completed. I refused to let the words "can't do" be in any soldier's vocabulary under my supervision. I instilled in them that if we failed our mission, our actions could get other soldiers killed. Furthermore, if we failed, it would take the Iraqi security forces more time to start taking over, defending and securing their own country.

Some of the soldiers and civilians working at Central Command were happy to see me when I came home, but others seemed jealous. I got much attention because the senior leadership wanted to know the good and the bad happening in Iraq. They wanted to know what I knew, and I had plenty of stories to tell them. So, for my month and a half in the States, I played the role of story teller, recounting what I had seen and had learned while overseas.

I barely had time to stop and realize how much better we had it here in this country, but it didn't take much awareness to look around and notice the difference between Baghdad and Tampa. While Tampa was not the most exciting city to me, it was far superior to the lifestyle of the people living in Baghdad. On the other hand, I have worked hard all of my life and enjoyed the long days that seemed so much more meaningful in the combat zone. I really did not miss the comforts of Tampa since the mission in Iraq seemed so much more important. After all, it was the terrorists who attacked us on 9/11, and I could not forget the events of that day. I guess you could say that I was somewhat brainwashed at that time.

Second Tour of Duty in Iraq

On January 4th, 2004, I was back in Iraq in a trailer in the International Green Zone. The trailers were all set up and managed by KBR (Kellogg, Brown and Root) the largest contractor for the United States Army. The trailer had its own shower, a single bed and a locker that I did not have previously. Of course, as I mentioned earlier, you only got a trailer when one became available. If the military didn't have space available, you had to fend for yourself.

There were several nights before getting the trailer that I slept on a couch in the palace. While this was not my choice of accommodations, a couch inside was better than sleeping in a tent, so I was obviously moving up when it came to accommodations. Although, sleeping on a couch in the palace had drawbacks too. People would roam the halls at all hours of the night making it impossible to get a good night of sleep.

Under Burka – Under Cover

Unlike most of the other military personnel, my job was not one I could do from behind a desk, so I went to the various facilities and locations where we were setting up warehouses with the necessary equipment. The goal was still to establish an operational logistical infrastructure that would support the police where they were being trained.

But I knew from the start that a blue-eyed, white American woman traveling through the streets of Baghdad would have been suicide on my part. The terrorists had a $25,000 bounty for killing an American male and a $250,000 bounty for killing an American female, or so I was told. They knew American sentiment and figured that chopping off the head of an American woman would be far more dramatic back in the United States if viewed on American television. So, with that in mind, I traveled wearing sunglasses and a burka.

A burka is a black face veil worn by Arabic women covering their entire face and body except for the eye holes through which they can see. Underneath, I had my uniform and flak vest on. I was also armed with a 9 millimeter and an AK-47. Since women were never seen driving themselves, I always had a male driving me, usually another soldier or a contractor, also in disguise. I generally rode in the back seat. Traveling around this way worked for me until I felt like it was getting too dangerous, which was around 2005. But that isn't to say there weren't close calls along the way.

I recall one incident where I was in the back of an old beat-up panel truck going from Baghdad to Taji, and a gas station had just been blown up by a car bomb in a roadside bombing. The U.S. Army Military Police had all of the traffic stopped. The contractor and Iraqi driver riding in the front of the truck wore head rags so they would not be identified as someone who was assisting the coalition.

There were about 200 Iraqis gathered around that scene, trying to figure out what had happened. Whenever a bombing occurred, they would all get curious and gather in the hot area, which I thought was kind of stupid. Even if they wanted to catch the car bombers, it would be quite unlikely because the bombers would hit and run very quickly before anyone would have the chance to catch them or even react. Terrorists did not normally stick around an attack zone for very long.

In hopes of getting us through the roadblock and on our way to Taji, I instructed my Iraqi driver to give the military police (MP) my military identification card. I thought they would just wave us through, and we could get out of there in the most expedient manner. But instead, the MPs came back to our vehicle with all of the Iraqis watching, who were curiously following the MPs. I'm thinking, *Oh my God, they're all pointing at the vehicle. They're going to get me killed.*

So when the MPs came back to the vehicle, I asked her,

"What are you trying to do ... get me killed? Just let us through." The sergeant let us through, and we got to Taji inside the perimeter, safe and sound once again.

While I was reasonably armed the entire two years I was in Iraq during the "Go to War on Terrorism" (GWOT) conflict, there was fortunately only one incident where I nearly had to fire one of my weapons against an unidentifiable Iraqi civilian.

There had been a bombing at the entrance to the International Green Zone, so they had all the traffic stopped. I was on a truck in my usual disguise with a senior executive service (SES) civilian, equivalent to a general officer. I worked with him very closely in late 2003 and early 2004. It was about 2300 hours (11 o'clock) at night, and we were trying to get into the Green Zone, but everyone was stopped outside the gate.

The MPs were doing the usual cleanup of the bomb attack area when an Iraqi man wearing a black trench coat started walking toward us. I first spotted him when he was about 300 feet away, and I yelled to him to stop, but he didn't understand, and even if he did, he didn't stop coming toward us. As he got closer, I moved my finger to the trigger of my weapon. Again, I yelled for him to stop, this time giving him a warning order that I was going to shoot him if he did not stop. My concern was that he had explosives on him under the trench coat.

Just as I was ready to pull the trigger, aiming at his leg and hoping that the shot wouldn't set off an explosive, he caught the attention of one of the MPs who came running over to him and yelled for him to stop. The MP grabbed him, put him on the ground and searched him to see if he had explosives or other types of weapons on him. As it turned out, he did not, so he was let go.

It was always very tense because you could not tell who the enemy was and who was friendly. Anyone who acted suspicious might be a terrorist. However, they did not even have to act suspicious to be the enemy. Unlike a war in which the soldiers wore different colored uniforms, this type of enemy just blended into the typical Iraqi crowd. This meant we always had to be on our toes and anticipate the worst.

Not being able to easily spot the enemy also made it difficult in the other area where I was involved, trying to re-open the airport.

During the air attacks in 2002, the entire airport complex had been blown to smithereens, so it was now being used for coalition military missions.

We were trying to get the airport back into the hands of the Iraqis, but it was slow going because it was still very dangerous, and some unfriendly RPG rockets had taken down some of our military aircraft over the past months. The military pilots knew how to dip and dive to avoid enemy fire while in flight, but this is not the way a commercial plane would want to carry passengers—trying to avoid enemy fire that would take down a plane in a split second. It took us time, but we had to do very careful security checks and background investigations to clear any Iraqi to enter the airport perimeter.

Surviving the Heat of the Battle

Whenever you left the Green Zone, you knew you were in constant danger. The more noticeable you were, the more danger you faced. For this reason, I was not thrilled about traveling as part of a twenty-truck military convoy that stuck out like a sore thumb or a giant moving target for whomever wanted to attack us. Although we had security vehicles with machine guns on top and others with sensing devices to pick up anything that got too close so it could be deactivated and disposed of, that did not stop convoys from being routinely attacked by the enemy.

When traveling in a convoy, I learned that the second vehicle, right behind security, was the least hit vehicle, so that's where I always tried to be. It seemed that the terrorists liked to hit more often in the rear of a convoy so they could get away quickly.

While starting out in one particular convoy, I was traveling with a couple of guys—a Marine who was driving and a civilian in the back seat. This time, I rode in the front seat since we were in a military convoy. As we pulled out into the convoy, another vehicle cut us off and pulled in front of us into the second position. I told my Marine buddy who was driving to jump in front of them, but he didn't want to make an issue out of it.

After we moved out of the Green Zone, we were traveling in an area of the town of Abu Graib known as suicide alley, which didn't make me feel safe in the slightest.

Suddenly, the vehicle that had pulled in front of us was hit by an inner explosive device (IED), which shattered all of its windows. The vehicle instantly caught fire, and the tires blew out, leaving the three passengers struggling to escape. We had been trailing ten feet behind the flaming SUV, and it was now traveling in our direction. John, the driver, did the only thing he could—he stepped on the accelerator and drove right through the flames to get on the other side of the attack zone. The Bradley tanks (armored tank vehicles) that roved suicide alley, immediately surrounded all of the remaining vehicles. The security forces rescued the passengers in the attacked vehicle, and we were all lead to a nearby camp for safety and security. There were three injured from the explosion but no casualties. The injured were given first aid as soon as we arrived.

We did try to vary the route and not establish a pattern by varying the times we traveled. It seemed that any military convoy always got lots of attention from the locals. I received my first Combat Action Badge from this attack.

There was another time something similar happened: we were moving equipment in a ten-trailer truck convoy with civilian security—mostly former cops, both British and American, making eight to ten thousand dollars a day on these dangerous assignments. We had moved only about three miles from the warehouse in Abu Graib, bound for Taji twenty-five miles away, when a truck in the convey hit a roadside IED. We immediately formed a circle around the convoy.

The driver of the blown-up vehicle was badly injured, so we called in a med-evac helicopter, which arrived to take him to the hospital shortly after. The driver, however, was an Iraqi, and I was not sure if the hospital set up by the coalition would treat an Iraqi. So, I jumped on the helicopter and went with him to the hospital to ensure he was taken care of by our hospital.

Shortly after we reached the hospital, I filled out a report for the record. I told the doctors that he was an

Iraqi working for the United States Army. They treated him, and I stayed with him for over 12 hours until they finally released him at about 11 o'clock that night.

I called a friend of mine in the Green Zone and asked if I could use a vehicle to drive the Iraqi to meet his family in downtown Baghdad. His home was on the other side of the 14th Street bridge—a bridge which took us over the Tigress River.

Baghdad, the capital city of Iraq, is surrounded by the Tigress and Euphrates rivers. Baghdad is essentially a little island in its own right. We had security guards on one side of the 14th Street bridge, while the other side was in the red zone. This meant that I had to travel into the red zone to get the Iraqi home. I hoped that his family were good guys and that I would not be identified by terrorists.

I got him home without an incident and figured I could drop him off without meeting the family for a late night snack. Although, I felt obligated to ensure he was taken care of since he was working for the U.S. Army when he was injured.

After dropping him off with his family, I turned around and headed back toward the 14th Street bridge at night, alone in the red zone.

This time, I wasn't as lucky as before; as it turned out, someone in a car parked on the side of the street spotted me, drove onto the road and started following me. The road wasn't exactly crowded at this time, so I took off, picking up speed while heading for the bridge. I figured if I could just get to the gate where the MP's were, they would see me and let me into the Green Zone. I drove like I was in the Indianapolis 500, scared for my life with the

149

other car in pursuit.

It did not take me long to get to the bridge and cross it before the other vehicle could catch me. The MPs saw me as I drove across and let me in the Green Zone without delay.

This was just another of numerous adventures where I knew my life was on the line while serving in Iraq.

Slow Mission Progress

The goal for us being in Iraq at this time was to secure, stabilize and build a government while also fighting terrorism. Experts were brought in to help the Iraqis establish a banking system, health care, a government and everything in between.

I bought the first five Iraq postage stamps from the new postal system for one dollar each, and I still have them in my possession today.

Essentially, lots of subject matter experts from the United States and Great Britain were headed to Iraq to help them establish things that they needed like banks, hospitals, police and fire stations, schools, post offices and other things we take for granted.

It was sad to see how so many of these people were living. In fact, it wasn't unusual to see Iraqi families living in garbage dumps, making homes out of rubbish and debris. I always thought their immune systems must've been very tolerable to bacteria and disease.

There was some change while I was there, but everything requiring change moved very slow and was ten times more difficult than you would expect.

I recall when the Iraqi people held the first election for prime minister. I was involved with the distribution and issuing of the weapons to support and protect that effort. Every designated voting location had to be guarded to ensure the safety of the people who chose to vote. The ballots also had to be closely watched to ensure the election was on the up and up.

One of the warehouses that I had established in Mosul, Northern Iraq, for receiving, issuing, and accounting for equipment for the police was used as a voting station.

After the election, this warehouse was used to store excess ballets and voting booths. It took months before I was able to get the election materials out of the warehouse and back to the contractors for its original planned purpose.

The airport was still an ongoing mission as we continued trying to resecure it so the Iraqis could have some commercial flights coming in and going out of there. They needed to bring in some revenue, and this was one possible solution. Although, insurance for carriers going in and out of Baghdad was too high for most commercial airlines to even consider.

After the air strike in 2002, the United States and collation forces were working very hard to rebuild Iraq. In fact, we were doing everything, and there were no jobs for the Iraqis. Many of them were now beggars while our soldiers were rebuilding their country. Some Iraqis found work at the airport, cleaning and doing other odd jobs, but employment was very hard to find for them. Although the Iraqi people had proven to be survivors, they were not accustomed to possessing much money during Saddam's regime. Most had gardens, grew chickens, and everything at the market place could be bought for pennies on our dollar. Their religion forbids them from eating pork, so they grew lots of chickens and half-bred sheep. When I left Iraq the last time in 2005, one dollar was equal to 1500 dinar.

As said before, progress was very slow. There just weren't enough soldiers to do what needed to be done. Plus, it was still very hard to be sure who was the enemy and who was friendly. You could train someone to be a cop and give him a weapon and a uniform, but you might never see him again. He could sell off the weapon or come back and use it against our soldiers as a terrorist.

It made progress very slow since we had to be very careful to screen everyone we were training. The language barrier was always an additional challenge as well unless you were lucky enough to have a translator.

If that didn't keep things moving at a slow pace, every time we got some momentum going, someone was sent back to the States. This was the case all over Iraq, making it very hard to move forward.

I found that it would take a tremendous amount of effort to set things up and establish a way of doing something, and just as we started moving forward, next thing I knew, I was back in Tampa, Florida at Central Command. It was very frustrating for me when I returned each time to see how many steps we had taken backward.

So, sure enough, as we tried to get a system in place, I was back in Tampa in August 2004, after my second tour of duty. This time, I was in Tampa for two months doing staff planning, going to meetings, writing-out plans and so on.

No longer was I telling stories of Iraq since many soldiers had returned by now and told their tales. Instead, I was doing what I considered boring staff work. I didn't really feel any sense of accomplishment, but it was where I was assigned, so I did my job the best way I could even though I still knew my job in Iraq was not done.

Although, I was starting to feel that my days were numbered in Iraq because I was so involved in what I was doing—getting out into the red zone and traveling around.

Word was getting out and about that there was this crazy American woman traveling all over Iraq in the red zones to Tikrit, Ar Ramadi, Babylon, Baghdad Police Academy, Taji, Bash Rah, and up and down Tampa road from Kuwait to Mosul. I'm sure I would have brought the terrorists a great bounty if they could have killed me off. Furthermore, I was helping the Iraqis establish police, border patrol, facility protective services; and of all things, a military.

I had started having nightmares of the terrorists capturing, raping and killing me after my return from Tampa in August of 2004, but I did not tell anyone at that time.

CHAPTER 8

MY LAST TOUR OF DUTY IN IRAQ

CHAPTER 8

MY LAST TOUR
OF DUTY IN IRAQ

It was October of 2004 when I returned to the theater of operations at the request of the general in charge of training and equipping the Iraq security forces. The leadership at Central Command felt I had already been over there long enough and didn't want me going back again. They wanted me to remain in Tampa, Florida. They felt they needed me to do staff work behind a desk for the logistics plans and operations division. The general in the theater, however, felt otherwise and managed to persuade the general officer that I worked for in Tampa that I was of significance to the operation and got things done that were critical to the fight against terrorism. He understood the value of continuity of operations and believed for the sake of such that I was of more value in Iraq.

Since I had an immense understanding of the logistics operation and infrastructure that I planned and developed, I agreed with the theater general without a doubt. I had also seen firsthand the problems and setbacks that come with rotations of personnel. I think he also knew that a large portion of the soldiers and contractors who went over to Iraq were not able to accomplish what I had been able to accomplish. This was largely because I was not afraid to take risks with my life. This was mainly because I refused to accept failure or allow the terrorists to intimidate me. After all, it was the terrorists who attacked the United States and killed innocent Americans on 9/11, and that attack still remained fresh on my mind, unforgettable and unforgivable.

In just the two months that I had been gone from Iraq, everything had become chaotic in the logistics operations for the Iraqi Army and other security forces. We had lost so much momentum, and I was amazed at how many steps we had taken backwards. I was asked to do an assessment of the logistics operations and identify problems for the general upon my return.

At that time, there was a lot of bickering going on between the chief of the wholesale operation (a retired Marine colonel) and the multi-national security forces for Iraq J-4 (a reserve colonel). The marine colonel had developed not only the wholesale logistics operations based on my plans that would support my retail operations, but he had also established a state of the art movement center where all registered movements could be monitored.

The purpose of this movement control center was to monitor convoys as they moved with supplies throughout Iraq. If a convoy were hit by a terrorist attack, we were able to see the episode immediately from the movement control center in Baghdad. This allowed the coalition forces to react with quick response and back up the friendly with more fire power and rescue any wounded.

The monitoring also helped to avoid what was called a blue on blue attack—that is, the coalition attacking other coalition forces.

Jack wanted to work with Randy by allowing one of the J-4's junior officers to work in the movement control center to ensure all convoys were registered and all 18 billion+ U.S. dollars worth of equipment was accounted for when in movement in the red zone at all times. On the other hand, the J-4 felt the retired Marine colonel was just trying to use one of his already shorthanded staffers.

In addition, the J-4 had two majors who were bypassing the accountability system by taking military 5-ton trucks to the Baghdad International Airport and moving the weapons, ammunition, uniforms and everything else purchased for the Iraqi Army to Taji, Iraq. The process for accountability became near to non-existent.

The manager of the wholesale warehouse, a lieutenant colonel in Abu Graib, caught the two majors loading trucks one morning two miles from the airport and gave them direct orders not to bypass the accountability system again. T

hey turned to walk away, but the lieutenant colonel was not finished with them, and I watched on. Regardless, that did not stop them until months late,r and Taji was a loss of property accountability nightmare. The majors went back to Baghdad IZ and informed the J-4 about the encounter with the lieutenant colonel. The J-4 called me and asked what had happened, and I told him that the lieutenant colonel was right in what he did, i.e., tried to maintain accountability of the supplies, weapons and ammunition. The J-4 said nothing more to me about the event, and I continued with my assessment.

After I briefed the general, with his chief of staff and J-4 in the room, I filled him in on some of the logistics problems. I told him that the J-4 needed to have a staff officer assigned to the movement control center, and all others should be trained there in order to understand the processes and procedures for convoy movement. I also told him about the accountability problems and the lack of payments to contractors for goods delivered. In addition, there was a lack of interaction between the wholesale and retail staffs. And lastly, I recommended that two of the J-4 staff officers be assigned to Baghdad International Airport to prevent the Iraqi customs officers from pilferage or theft of the supplies purchased for the Iraqi Army.

Meanwhile, a lot of contractors were providing services, equipment and support to the operation, and many of them had fallen into financial troubles. They were not getting paid because no one was keeping track of the supplies coming in, where they were going and whether or not they had actually arrived at their destination. One of the biggest problems our military had was this lack of continuity. A coalition soldier would rotate out of the theater, leave a job in many cases, and nobody would take over that job and keep it going. So, I had my work cut out for me with over 3,000 invoices and claims from contractors waiting for payment.

Logistics includes a great deal of documentation and follow-up to see that things are done as expected. This was not at all being taken care of while I was not there.

I had the unenviable task of straightening out the mess. To do so, I had to physically contact the service providers from the information provided on the original contracts, and, in most cases, I didn't have a clue as to who ordered what or where it went. I had to get proof that whatever was supposed to be sent to Baghdad actually got there and that someone received it and signed for it. As a result, a lot of small businesses went bankrupt because they were waiting for their money. So, I had to put all of the documentation together, and then if there was enough to justify the payment, I would take it to the finance officer, and he would get these contractors paid.

To clean up this mess and get things caught up where they should be, it took me two months of working day and night. And this was just my first assignment during my final tour of duty in the combat zone.

Meanwhile, I was also trying to get my own logistics operation up and running once again. One of he problems was that too many of our people were over-tasked, and others were simply not doing their jobs. For every one person whom you could trust to get a job done, there were ten you could not rely on and who were just there to do their time, stay safe and get back home as soon as possible.

It would have been great if we could have turned a lot of the rebuilding work over to the Iraqis since, after all, it was their country, and they needed work. However, the Iraqis didn't get it. They had no system in place for doing any of this, so we (the coalition) had to handle the entire operation in the early years of the war.

What made it even more difficult was that when we did seek out Iraqi help, we still did not know the good guys from the bad. So it took us some time to do security and background checks before allowing Iraqi involvement.

It was also difficult to get the basics that we needed, even enough food at times. Kellogg, Brown and Root (KBR) had a contract to provide dining facilities where the majority of meals were prepared and served. The food was coming in to the airport or moved by convoy from Kuwait, then distributed throughout Iraq to coalition camps.

My boss at Central Command was assigned as the J-4—the chief for logistics at Central Command—and had overall responsibility for transportation, which is a function of logistics. There was not enough aircraft to support all operations, so the CCJ4 had to establish priorities. This is one of the reasons why a lot of the stuff was trucked on through Kuwait to Iraq. It was a challenge to get all the supplies we needed for forces and a challenge for me to complete my assignment of stocking the warehouses in Iraq with the necessary equipment.

Trouble at Taji Depot

In January 2005, I moved to the Abu Graib wholesale operations, traveling with convoys and continuing to identify problems in the logistics wholesale and retail operations. I had now acquired the general's ear and had gained his trust in my ability to assess and fix problems.

On the 12th of January, the chief of staff sent a message to me and requested that I go to Taji. The senior staff wanted an assessment of the problems at the wholesale operations in support of the Iraqi Army. A convoy was scheduled to travel to Taji two days later, and I would be on it.

Needless to say, the convoy was hit by an IED two miles outside Abu Graib. The Iraqi driver in the third vehicle of the convoy had major head wounds and had to be medical evacuated to the hospital in Baghdad. I elected to go along with him, provide comfort as best I could and ensure he received the medical attention he needed from the coalition hospital.

When I finally got to Taji on the 5th of February 2005, I quickly became frustrated with the lack of manpower to do the job. To make matters worse, all of the soldiers were tired, overworked and disgruntled. They had been mistreated and abused by a couple of majors who preceded me. Oh yes, these were the same two majors who were taking equipment from the Baghdad International Airport without accountability.

In an effort to better understand what was going on, I did group counseling as soon as I got to Taji with the twelve soldiers, followed by face-to-face, one-on-one counseling with each of the soldiers. I told them that they could say anything they wanted, and there would be no repercussions.

A couple of young female soldiers told me that they had been threatened with reprimands and having their ranks taken away if they did not do as they were told. Other soldiers also had complaints about these two majors. I told them that as long as I was there, if they had any problems with either of these majors, they should let me know, and I would take care of it.

Fortunately, we had no more difficulties with the majors after that. Since I had the general's support, they knew not to cross me or the soldiers under my care.

When I first arrived in Taji, there was no place for me to stay. This was not the first time I had to fend for myself. The military had not provided me with housing, so I was essentially left on my own to find living accommodations.

For a while, I was living in my car. Fortunately, in Taji, there were men's and women's bathrooms set up with showers as well as laundries where you could get your clothes cleaned, so it wasn't too bad. Most all of my needs were met, and I had the time to work eighteen to twenty hours a day and slowly get the operation on track.

In late 2004, the contractor's regional manager responsible for building the retail warehouses ordered a trailer, which, when it arrived, did not meet his specifications. The Iraqi-American who provided the trailer gave it to me after he could not get paid from the contractor and after he was discovered by a terrorist as a supporter to the Americans.

This Iraqi-American who had access to the local market was held in one of Saddam's prison camps in 2003, accused of being a spy for the U.S. and was placed on death row. After the war started in 2003, he was released from Saddam's custody along with others held in prison camps. Now, the terrorists had identified him as an Iraqi helping the United States, threatened his life and the lives of his family members who lived in Baghdad. He fled to safety in Jordan with his family and left everything behind, including the trailer he gave to me. I appreciated him giving me the trailer, and from March until the end of September, when I left Iraq for the final time, I lived in and possessed the trailer.

I lived in the trailer on the depot without security

because I did not want to jeopardize the security of the $18 billion of equipment for which I was responsible.

Each night, I worked on statements of work for the depot and drove the perimeter with my Iraqi counterpart between 2300 hours (11:00 p.m.) and 0300 hours (3:00 a.m.) to ensure terrorists were not trying to get inside. Each night, I slept a few hours curled up with my AK-47.

My soldiers and I worked at the Taji Depot for two months to get the equipment gathered up and secured. I had the twenty-six warehouses renovated at the Taji depot and put inventory in almost each and every one. I worked with a retired Marine colonel who got a modification to his contract so I could get an automated inventory system called "EXCEED" in place. We also got help from the military police to get most of the stolen vehicles back that should have been stored for the Iraqi military. They put up roadblocks, stopped drivers who were riding around in the vehicles and confiscated them.

I tried to accomplish as much as possible. My communications training was paying off as I had twenty-one Internet drops as well as telephones installed and satellite communications set up at the depot. I developed a functional staff with the soldiers I had been assigned. I established operations, supply shipping and receiving sections in addition to inventory management who maintained property accountability. I developed the plans and statements of work for communication connectivity so we could communicate with Baghdad where the program managers resided, who purchased all of the equipment.

Every day was a surprise in regard to what we were to ship or what we would receive, but, including the on-going night missions, there was never a dull moment.

The J-4 staff would send a shipping order, and we would load the trucks or helicopters and ship wherever we were directed to. We also loaded emergency cargo when necessary to support on-going operations or planned attacks such as Fallujah.

Fallujah was a known harbor for terrorists. The civilians in Fallujah were given advance warning to evacuate, but some did not. As a result, when the strike wiped out the city of Fallujah, some were killed during the operation. The decision to stay after the warning was a matter of choice by those who would not leave.

We did a lot at the Taji depot considering I had just the twelve soldiers for the first couple of months to work with, but there was so much more that could have been done if we had sufficient manpower.

The Taji Challenge

Slowly but surely, we reached a point where the Iraqis had started taking over a lot more responsibilities that were being handled by the American and British troops. Iraqi soldiers were now taking charge of handling many of the incoming supplies. Although, unfortunately, they were also stealing things left and right.

In Iraq, the common way of Iraqi thinking was that if you had something in your possession, then it was yours, regardless of how you got it in the first place. In fact, when I returned to Iraq, there were 300 to 400 missing vehicles that were supposed to be locked up in warehouses until issued and accounted for. These vehicles were being used by everyone and anyone who could get a set of keys. The situation was totally out of control.

There were a lot of problems in Taji where we had set up wholesale operations for the Iraqi military. Equipment was scattered all over the base, unaccounted for and unsecured in February 2005. There were not enough people whom we could trust to take care of securing the equipment, and there was simply not enough coalition staff to do this job. Even some of the people we thought we knew did not help the situation.

For example, one of the warehouses had numerous breaches where ammunition and weapons were stolen. The lieutenant colonel in charge of the ammunition supply point had been storing weapons and compatible ammunition in the same warehouse, which is definitely not a smart idea, nor is it operationally sound. Ammunition and weapons should be stored in separate locations, so, if someone did break in, they would not be armed and dangerous when they left.

Of course, once the situation was pointed out, it should have been immediately corrected. It wasn't! The general in charge of the Iraqi military training followed up with a staff visit soon after the third breach and theft of weapons, after which, he sent me an e-mail directing me to relieve the officer in charge of ammunition and weapons by sending him to Baghdad. I was told to let him know that he was going home because he didn't fix the problem or take an active role to stop the loss of weapons and ammunition, in other words, derelict of duty.

In the military, and in most businesses for that matter, once you identify a problem, you have to fix it or you get sent home.

I ended up with the responsibility of securing not only the weapons and ammunition, but also twelve, forty-foot containers of vehicle repair parts that were delivered at the same time. I had to establish priorities due to the manpower shortage, so repair parts would have to wait even though the J-4 sent a message telling me I had five days to complete the parts inventory.

I acquired an additional five soldiers who were assigned to the ammunition supply point. That was not close to the number of soldiers I needed for the task I had been assigned. The now seventeen soldiers and I worked 24/7 for three days and nights to separate the ammunition from weapons. We also had to continue our normal operations of shipping and receiving. This all became a major, major operation and somewhat overwhelming, but the soldiers and I did the best we could under the conditions, limitations and circumstances.

Once we got everything secured, we stacked the forty-foot container boxes in front of the doors of the warehouses to prevent theft. It took a crane to move the containers, and this was the only way anyone could move them if they wanted to get into the warehouse.

By the time we were finished, we were all totally exhausted. I gave all the soldiers a day off to rest and recoup, and that was all the time I could stand down without jeopardizing the logistics missions.

My Dirty Dozen, Plus Five

There was a lot of work to be done in the rebuilding and renovating, and I had now had my original dirty dozen plus five soldiers from the Ammunition Supply

Point (ASP). I had now gained eleven Iraqi soldiers and contractors who would attempt a massive undertaking. As a leader, you quickly recognize who you can depend on to get the job done, and those individuals are who you become reliant on regardless of their rank.

The Iraqis were not allowed in the ammunition storage area. The situation: run-down, substandard warehouses that were dirty and contaminated, some destroyed from air strikes, and in dire need of renovation.

I worked hard with every night the same—three to four hours of sleep and many late nights. I recognized the need to put together a briefing to determine how many people would be needed to run an operation the size of a wholesale depot.

In my mind, the Iraqis needed to do more and start sharing more responsibility as well as understanding how a wholesale warehouse operation works.

In the States, an operation the size of Taji would have over 3,000 people doing the work. In addition to many tasks I had at Taji, I also had to continue identifying and writing statements of work for what we needed to progress forward.

The Iraqi Minister of Defense came to Taji to review the personnel requirements and, after some discussion, accepted my plans. We determined it would take 330 additional soldiers to run this depot level operation. There was no room for slugs, and everyone worked extremely hard. I had factored in contract manpower at around 1,200 employees. As I mentioned earlier, I now had seventeen soldiers to do this job, and again, this was an 18 billion dollar operation.

Recruiting the Iraqis to help us was also difficult. They were not trained, and teaching them took increased time and effort. By the time I left Iraq, eight months later, we were just about where we needed to be with enough personnel to do the work and gaining momentum every day. By this point, there were also more than 800 contractors in Taji depot alone.

It was around May of 2005 when one of the battalions in Taji started supporting our efforts by allowing twenty additional soldiers to work depot operations during the day. This came after a staff visit by one of the support division commanders—a two star. We were doing all sorts of things—reconstructing warehouses, building a dining facility for the new Iraqi soldiers (so they could eat their own types of foods), building firehouses, a medical supplies storage warehouse, and a communication infrastructure including drops for telephones and Internet. I was the only one writing the requirement statements of work because I found that by the time I edited one of the junior officer's or enlisted soldier's writings, I might as well have done it myself. So, the late nights were finally paying off.

Pitfalls – Frustration

When I look back at the overall picture, as I saw it, we needed more troops, dedicated troops, and longer tours of duty. Initially, tours of duty were three months, which wasn't enough time to understand, much less set up operations or get anything accomplished.

After about a year, the tours of duty changed to six months, which was better, but still not enough time to implement a plan and see a job through to the end. Eventually, the tours were extended to one year, which is more realistic to mission success.

In my opinion, tours of duty should have been one year from the start. In logistics, you need time to plan, get an operation up and running, and then sustain operations. You then need time to iron out the kinks and make sure it is running smoothly with property accountability, which entails training soldiers. In three or six months, this was virtually impossible. "You can't even learn a job in three months," continued to be my argument. You'd just get started, and then you were transferred back to the States. Each time I returned, I walked in to a mess that needed to be straightened out. We needed a much better sense of continuity, and it could not be achieved with short rotations.

Of course, what made it more difficult in the rebuilding stage was that the war was not over. Typically, rebuilding might take place after a war ends and when there has been truce called or a treaty signed. In this case, we were trying to build an infrastructure in a nation that was still unstable, with terrorists blowing up pipelines, buildings and the like as quickly as we could build them. Everything took ten times as long and was ten times more difficult because whenever you left the Green Zone, you could've been killed, so precautions were necessary, and your guard always had to be up. Not surprisingly, you had to be very careful about where you moved outside the Green Zone.

The result of short tours of duty and the danger of leaving the Green Zone was that you would get people who didn't really want to be in Iraq. They would go to

171

work, do as little as possible for three or six months then go home. They took no risks, got very little results, and you couldn't necessarily report these soldiers to the higher-ranking officers because often the top was part of the incompetence, excluding the generals. It was happening in the logistics field quite often at O-6 level and below with military personnel trying to coast their way through and stay out of the red combat zone.

For example, one Colonel was assigned to the IZ in Baghdad and promised his wife he would not travel outside of the Green Zone. You can't do anything effectively in logistics in a combat zone by simply sitting at a desk, or so I thought. But somehow this colonel managed to avoid going outside the Green Zone, but he did manage to get his butt chewed out routinely by the General. You can't build an infrastructure without some hands on experience; it doesn't matter what your assignment is in the world.

Another issue we dealt with was contractors on the battlefield. The Army wrote a policy in 2001-2002 that allowed contractors on the battlefield. This was, in my opinion, one of the worst policies that the Army has ever approved. On the other hand, I see the logic of trying to fill the gap caused by the cut of eight divisions during the Democratic administration in the 90's. That cut in military forces has cost the U.S. government dearly.

There were three types of contractors. First, there were those who genuinely wanted to do the right thing and make a difference. Then there were those who were there for the sake of making a buck, and finally there were the Iraqi contractors who were not at the same level as the Americans in terms of being able to do the jobs and having the same quality of materials available. This was unfortunate because they needed the work. However, they could not compete with the American and British contractors.

The biggest problem were those contractors in the second group—those who were there only to make money—some of them were American and some British.

We ended up spending so much more money on people who were not looking out for our troops. Truck drivers who didn't even complete high school were making $80,000 tax free annually by taking advantage of the situation because we desperately needed to have materials transported from a lack of internal transportation capability. Considering that dedicated and disciplined soldiers were making $35,000 and putting themselves in harm's way every day, it was very hard to accept contractors taking advantage of the situation. Their priority was the money and not always getting the mission done. If you needed them to do something to help the overall effort, it was too easy for them to say, "That's not my job." They made their own rules, and, in the middle of a war, that's also very hard to accept; but they were protected within the scope of their work. It was hard to see soldiers dying and contractors protected by those same soldiers.

I was told it took four soldiers to protect one contractor in the combat zone. Is this crazy or what? As if fighting a war was not enough to ask of our soldiers, now they were babysitters for contractors.

One of the most frustrating things about the Iraq war was that the coalition forces would build something, and it would get blown up shortly after—especially the oil refineries and the pipelines. This was still going on when I left in October 2005. It was important for us to build the oil refineries since it was the Iraqi government's main source of revenue. Our job was to help build their infrastructure so that they could have a means of helping finance the war effort and rebuild their country.

We had experts in finance and banking come in to teach the Iraqis about finance and how money should be controlled, recorded and managed. Trying to teach the Iraqis anything was like teaching babies how to walk. After all, prior to 2003, Saddam controlled everything. He was even the Minister of Finance, Minister of Security, and Minister of Forces ... the minister of all ministries.

For me, the warehouses were my primary concern, and preventing them from being blown up was only half the battle. Getting the equipment accounted for and safely into the warehouses was the other major concern. We were trying to decentralize logistics within the country (which has twenty-eight provinces) so that everything did not have to go through Baghdad, which was how Saddam Hussein had controlled everything, i.e., centralized control.

The coalition had convoys going out into the combat areas every day with truckloads of equipment including weapons for the retail logistics and training sites. It was not at all uncommon for the trucks to be attacked during movement.

During some of the logistics convoy attacks, the security forces (mostly civilians) were known to leave the attack area and leave the supplies behind, which would inevitably fall into the hands of the terrorists.

Final Departure From Iraq

If I'd had a crystal ball and knew that two seeming-ly-innocent activities on my part when leaving Iraq could have caused me so much grief, I would have done things very differently. That is, if I had not been suffering from combat fatigue, combat stress and sleep deprivation when I left Iraq, I would have taken better care of myself and less care for the mission, and perhaps I would have not taken a seemingly-innocent trip to Thailand.

I still do not understand why selling the trailer was a crime since it was not uncommon for personnel to sell personal belongs to others when leaving the theater. My attorney told me that the crime was not that I sold the trailer, but it was a crime that I sold it to the contractor whom I sold it to. Too bad someone did not tell me that at the time.

I would be leaving Iraq the first few days of October, so I had to start thinking about what to do with any belong-ings I could not take with me, which obviously included my trailer. So, shortly before I was finally ready to go, I hung a "for sale" sign in the window.

I got two responses, one of which was from the con-tractor's manager with whom I had been working in 2003-04. He was willing to pay my asking price of $4,000 for the trailer. We needed someone at Taji to support retail logistics for the Iraqi Highway Patrol. I thought by selling the trailer to this contractor, it would put personnel in place sooner to expedite the support to the Iraqi Highway Patrol.

My goal was always to accomplish a mission, and while I was in Iraq, all missions to which I was assigned were always completed. A mission was typically to receive supplies, load and unload cargo, account for the supplies, build a logistics infrastructure, get supplies shipped out on time, and make sure the cargo got to where it needed to be safely. This included loading helicopters, as previously stated, often at night for critical missions.

My philosophy was that we would never miss a mission, and we didn't. To ensure every mission was completed and that we continued to build the logistics infrastructure, it was not uncommon for me to go many nights with little or no sleep.

After I left the combat zone, I stayed in touch with one sergeant who was a very hard worker. Whatever I would ask this guy to do, he would get it done. I could always depend on him regardless of how difficult the task might be.

He arrived in Iraq in May of 2004, having volunteered to return to Iraq when he found out I was coming back in October of 2004. He wanted to work with me, and we have always maintained a mutual respect.

When I left Iraq for the last time, he had three months left on his assignment. He later told me that the lieutenant colonel who took my place did not meet many of the missions. Sometimes he found it impossible to do so, but I am sure he did not lose a night of sleep, or go the extra mile. I was also told that after I left and the lieutenant colonel who was left to fill my shoes at Taji failed, the job was filled by a general officer.

Missing a mission was just not acceptable to me, because if you missed a mission, you could put our soldiers at risk. The supplies were also critical to the training and retail sites missions, as well as getting the Iraqis equipped so they could take over and defend their own country, and removing our own soldiers from harm's way.

Selling the trailer was simply part of preparing to leave Iraq. It was advertised to anyone who wanted to buy it. So, unknown to me, I sold it to this particular contractor, which made the sale a crime. This does not make sense to me since I believe it should not have mattered whom I sold it to. All contracts had been selected by the Joint Contracting Command long before I was leaving Iraq, and I was not the person authorizing the contracts. I was never a contracting officer and did not have the training or authority to authorize contracts.

The Department of Justice claimed that the sale of the trailer constituted a bribe, which was ludicrous because there was no advance planning to sell it to him or anyone for that matter. It was an overnight decision to get rid of something that was given to me and was not the property of the United States government. Then, the DOJ claimed the trailer belonged to the U.S. Army. There is nothing farther from the truth then or now as I have since been prosecuted and served my sentence.

When I finally left Taji on the 1st of October, 2005, en route to Baghdad International Airport, by way of an Apache helicopter, I thought I could finally get some sleep. I had not taken leave in 130 days, so rest and relaxation (R&R) was very much needed before returning to Central Command in Tampa.

I made plans to go to Thailand with the wife of the contractor with whom I had worked. She was a very nice person whom I had come to know well. Innocently on my part, as she was a Thai national, and I thought it would be nice to go with someone who spoke the language and knew her way around the country.

She made frequent trips to Thailand because she still had family over there, and I thought it would give me time to get some badly-needed rest. It would also be a new experience, an opportunity to meet the Thai nationals and see another part of the world. So, we planned the trip in September shortly before I left. We planned our departure from Kuwait for Thailand on the 4th of October.

As it turned out, I wasn't able to relax quite yet; I needed to get a flight out of Iraq and go to Kuwait City. From there, I would go to Qatar, where Central Command was located, to hand in my weapon, which was mandatory.

The first problem I encountered was that I couldn't get a flight out of Iraq. It took me two days to get out of Baghdad International Airport. Unlike the United States, there were no local accommodations or airport hotels, nor did the airport have comfortable couches to lie down on, so I slept on the ground at the airport with one eye open but did not get any more than two hours of sleep.

The problem with sleeping while waiting for an outbound flight is that you may not hear your name when called, you could miss your departure. Thus, sleeping at the airport could be fatal. I learned that "No Doze" and "Red Bull" really do work, but they're probably not very healthy to use too frequently!

Finally, after two days and nights of waiting, I was manifested on a flight to Kuwait but not Kuwait City, where I needed to go. The flight landed at Ali Al Salem, a military air base somewhere in northern Kuwait at 0200 hours (2:00 a.m.). Still no sleep or rest! By now, the lack of sleep had noticeably taken a toll on my mental state of awareness.

I was very tired and running behind schedule since the plan was for me to turn in my weapon at another Southwest Asian (SWA) country and for us to head to Thailand on the fourth. So, I called the contractor who was in Kuwait, woke him up at around 0600 hours (6 a.m.) and asked him if he would please come and get me at this airport in Kuwait and drive me to Kuwait City, which he did.

Finally, I was in Kuwait City at the commercial airport and ready to head to Central Command Forward. The next problem to arise was that I had my weapon on me and had to go through airport security. I had traveled in the United States with a weapon before. As long as you take the weapon apart and separate the weapon from the ammunition, you could check a weapon with no problems. Also, being military personnel with valid identification, I assumed I would not have a problem checking my weapon to the other SWA country. The same rules, however, did not apply in Kuwait, where they took the weapon, and I was detained.

So, once again, I used the phone to call the contractor, who once again came to help me out. He had been in Kuwait for fifteen years and was well known in Kuwait City, so they let me go with him and keep my weapon, which I would soon turn in when I finally got to Central Command Forward in Qatar.

There were shuttle buses from the military airport in this Southwest Asian country for military personnel going to and from Central Command Forward, which made things easier.

Finally, when it was time to leave Central Command Forward and return to Kuwait City, I had yet another seven hour wait for a flight, which I was on the next morning.

By the time I arrived back in Kuwait City, it was October 4, the day we were leaving for Thailand. Needless to say, my body was working in overdrive, and I had reached an unbelievable level of physical and mental exhaustion.

Next, I had to go to the office where the contractor was and close any payments that were hanging loose, i.e., payments due from the U.S. Army that had not been paid for services received.

I checked my e-mails and went to the contractor's home where his wife was waiting for me, pleased that I was going to accompany her on one of her trips to Thailand. While I was at their home, waiting for our flight departure time, I took the opportunity to sleep for a few hours until it was time to go to an airport, yet again.

When we left for the airport, I was still under the assumption that I would purchase my ticket when I got to the check-in counter. I knew that the reservations had been made but had no idea that the tickets had already been purchased.

The contractor, however, unbeknown to me, had taken time off from his office to take his wife and me to the airport. He parked the car and came inside the terminal with his wife and me. Surprisingly, he pulled two tickets from his pocket and handed one to me for the flight. I said, "I can't take this ticket," but he insisted and said they were non-refundable. He's the kind of guy who won't take no for an answer.

He told me it was nothing more than his way of show-ing gratitude for my help with getting the retail logistics operation established. In other words, it was his way of saying thanks. I had no fight left in me at that time.

Looking back, I shouldn't have taken the ticket, but I was simply worn down and was not capable of anything other than sleep. I was suffering from severe sleep depri-vation, combat stress, and combat fatigue and just did not have it all together. What my mind and body was expe-riencing at that time is unimaginable to those who have never been in combat or suffered from sleep deprivation. So, with this ticket in hand, I boarded a flight to Thailand with the contractor's wife and slept the entire way.

To be honest, I don't remember getting on board the plane in Kuwait. Regardless, a friend of the wife picked us up at the airport, and as soon as I got in the car, I once again went to sleep. We were headed for a town called Padi, where the hotel reservations had been made and again, to my surprise, paid for by the contractor's wife.

I had my own room at the hotel while the contractor's wife and her friend shared a room. I slept the rest of that day and night and most of the entire next day until about 4 p.m. (30 hours straight).

It was now October 6, and I headed outside to find the contractors wife and her friend by the pool. They wanted to go out that night to a local club that had music and food. So we went to the club at around 6:30 p.m., had dinner and listened to the music, which was pretty good even though I could not understand what they were say-ing. Around 9:30 p.m., we returned to the hotel, and, you guessed it, I crashed, falling into a deep sleep once again.

The long hours, stress, lack of sleep, and too many missions to support with not enough staff to do the work had worn me down during my months in Taji, Iraq. I was clearly exhausted and was slowly but surely recovering from the months of lost sleep in a part of the world where bombings and other acts of terror rocked the night, and the constant need to support our troops limited my time for rest.

Before leaving Thailand, on the fourth day of my visit, we returned to the capital city, Bangkok, where the hotel bill was once again prepaid. We stayed for two nights, did some shopping and took in the city sites.

Before I left, I bid my friend farewell. She stayed in Thailand after my departure to visit her grandmother and brother, and I returned to Kuwait City where I had left some of my personal belongings.

It was a five day trip, from the 4th through the 9th of October, during which I spent the majority of the time sleeping. I had accrued more than enough time for leave and was now ready to return to the United States. What I didn't know upon returning from this brief trip was that no matter how long I had served my country, how hard I had worked, how diligent I was or how many times I put my life in danger to protect and support our troops, I would be punished for taking this trip.

As I mentioned earlier, I probably should not have taken the ticket. I knew nothing about this trip being paid for until I reached the airport in Kuwait and was ready to leave.

As a side note, I later researched the trip on the Internet

and found that the cost to me would have been around $3,000. The DOJ, in the estimated cost of their claims against me, raised that number to $5,000.

I told them and showed my attorney the numbers, and he said that it did not matter. The fact of the matter is that I received the ticket. Either way, it begs the question, why would I have sacrificed my career, my pride, integrity and solid reputation for a $5,000 trip and $4,000 received for selling the trailer? It just doesn't pass the common sense test that I would throw everything away for $9,000.

I will not say at this point that I am not guilty of anything that I was accused of. I will leave that decision to anyone who reads my story and chooses to judge me. I know what I did, what I did not do and what my intentions were while in Southwest Asia. Anyone's judgment against me does not matter to me anymore. I can look at myself in the mirror and know who I am. I can hold my head high and be proud of that regardless of the label I have been given.

CHAPTER 9

LIFE AFTER THE STORM

Chapter 9

Life After the Storm

Life has been difficult for me because I am my own worst enemy when it comes to judgment. The trauma of 9/11, the combat, and the DOJ prosecution still haunts me as if it were yesterday. I am working on letting go of the past and trying to look to the future.

I did manage to save my military retirement and veteran's benefits through the plea bargain. I gave a guilty plea in return to save what I had worked for for over thirty years, and I am using my VA education benefits to continue my studies for a PhD.

The first doctor whom, I had had with the VA, Dr. Anna Modesto, was one amazing lady when working with me and the PTSD. I went from constantly crying with suicidal thoughts to understanding how to compartmentalize traumatic events. The VA doctors have also prescribed the appropriate medication to manage my sleep deprivation and depression.

It was Dr. Modesto who thought a dog would be good for me. I got a teacup chihuahua whom I do not know how to live without. Dr. Modesto is also credited with my ambition to write a book. She thought it would be good therapy; although, it has taken several years because some parts of it triggered deep depression and reminded me of the past. The VA has been my saving grace who has been on call for me 24/7.

I remain secluded from society and only have a few friends whom I meet with on occasion. My chihuahua, Buffy, is and has been my constant companion. She is without a doubt a blessing sent from heaven.

As a result of the regular counseling at the VA, I think I am ready to speak to some groups that my current doctor thinks would be interested in my story—for example, other female veterans who served in the combat zone and are struggling with post-traumatic stress disorder.

My probation officer has indicated that he will petition the court for an early release from probation because I have done well with staying in compliance with the rules, regulations and directives. The ordered probation period was three years, so if the court approves an early release, I could be done with the prosecution this year (2014).

It bothers me that I gave thirty years of my life in defense of this country, and now, I am not even allowed to vote. Many take the privilege to vote for granted and do not show up at the ballet. It's like that for many things in life—they are not important until you don't have them any longer.

As I write this last chapter, I can only ask that those who do not know me or have never met me should not judge me. I am not the person the press painted me to be, nor am I the person written about on many Internet blogs. I am a person who can look in the mirror, know what I did and did not do, and still hold my head up and be proud of that person looking back. I still have my retirement and my VA benefits, and for that, I am thankful.

I don't believe in our government any longer, especially the justice system. This is a result of my experience. I always thought you were innocent until proven guilty. *WRONG!* Before I was questioned the first time, they believed me to be guilty, and the burden of proof regarding my innocence was up to me.

As you can see, I am not over the prosecution. I find myself always looking over my shoulder in fear. The prosecution had such a traumatic affect on me after serving multiple combat tours and will be with me until the day I die. I have felt such betrayal that I don't think I can ever trust again.

I do pray to God to help me find the good in the trauma that I have encountered over the past fourteen years, and show me how to help others who can learn from my experiences.

Afterword

One of my associates wrote this message to me after I took a guilty plea:

"Upon reading your guilty plea knew it was the result of government intimidation, etc. Under the circumstances, I certainly do not blame you, but sadden as many others who really knew you, the overall dedicated efforts you put forth in a time of war, life threatening situations you placed yourself with sole objective being to see the mission successfully accomplished. To have you subjected to such misinformation, mistreatment, situation you are now confronted, etc., one can only wonder how justice can be so blind. We became victims of government actions trying to pit us against one another, using, forcing others to say what they wanted to secure indictments while many of the real culprits roam free. Whatever happens, my respect, prayers will always be with you and eventually the real truth will someday be known."

~Anonymous

ABOUT THE AUTHOR

Born in 1954, Levonda Joey Selph experienced the hardships of growing up in a life of poverty where she learned a strong work ethic from her father, which would influence her positively as she grew older. At the age of twenty-four, she decided to join the military to get away from the difficulties she was faced with, as well as a chance to travel and acquire an education.

This proved to be just what she was looking for, and, during the thirty years she was there, she moved up the military ladder. First in the US Air Force and then in the US Army, she earned several certificates of achievement, thirty-seven decorations and awards, a commission presented by Senator John McCain, and two bronze stars. She was promoted to full bird colonel in addition to earning a Bachelor's degree in Business Management and a Master's degree in Adult Education during that time.

Being no stranger to the military danger in war-ravaged countries, she spent time in South Korea and Iraq and was deployed to Desert Storm as well. Needless to say, she experienced many of the things that we only read or hear about in the news up close and in person. No matter where she served, it was always to serve her country and safeguard the lives of soldiers under her care.

In spite of her difficulties, and not to be defeated, she is currently working toward her PhD in Leadership and Management.